#1 *NEW YORK TIMES* BESTSELLER

TONY ROBBINS

"A gold mine of moneymaking information!"
— **STEVE FORBES**
Forbes magazine

MONEY
MASTER THE GAME

7 SIMPLE STEPS TO FINANCIAL FREEDOM

SECRETS FROM THE WORLD'S GREATEST FINANCIAL MINDS

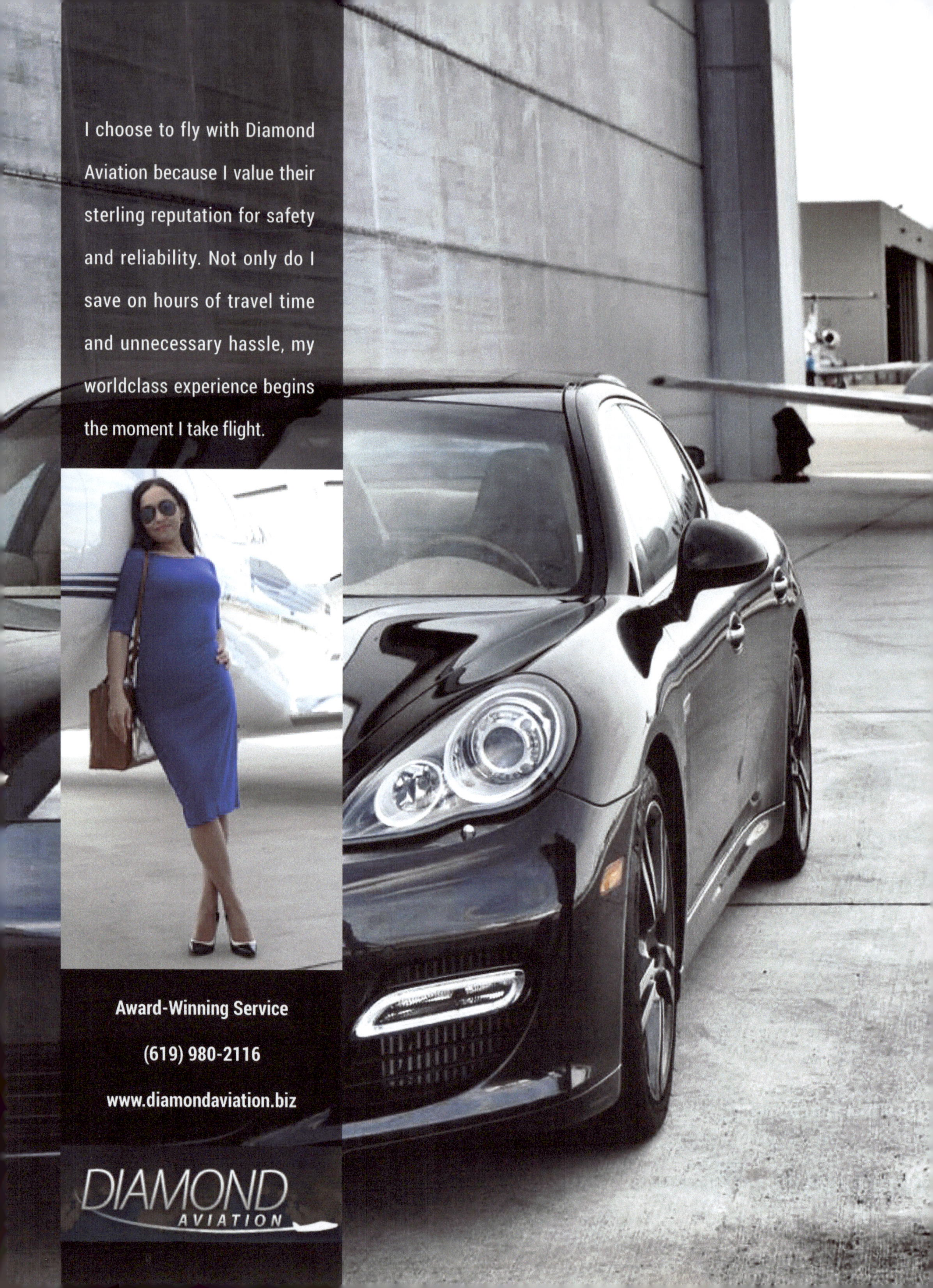

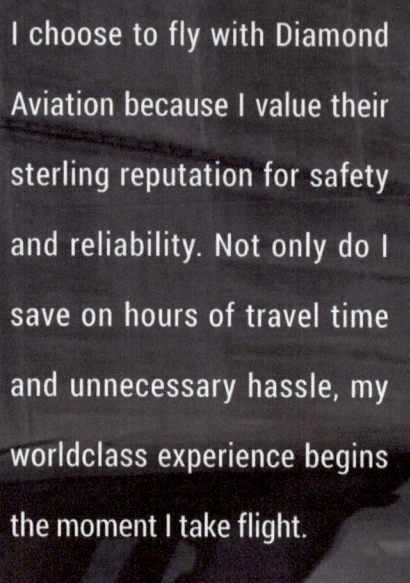

"I choose to fly with Diamond Aviation because I value their sterling reputation for safety and reliability. Not only do I save on hours of travel time and unnecessary hassle, my worldclass experience begins the moment I take flight."

Award-Winning Service

(619) 980-2116

www.diamondaviation.biz

DIAMOND
AVIATION

#WORLDCLASS

WWW.WORLDCLASSMAGAZINES.COM

EDITOR-IN-CHIEF
Katrina Starzhynskaya

EXECUTIVE EDITOR
Jennifer Niskanen

EDITOR
Jennifer Peterson

CONTRIBUTING WRITERS
Lou Altman • Lee Parore • Marie Delcioppo • Derek Henry • Michael B. Asimor

DESIGNER
Reena DKL

ADVERTISING INFORMATION
888-520-5532
info@worldclassmagazines.com

EDITORIAL SUBMISSION
info@worldclassmagazines.com

FOR MORE INFORMATION VISIT:
www.worldclassmagazines.com

contents

JOHN ELLSWORTH
PROMOTING SPORTS AND MENTAL TOUGHNESS

Pg 01

DR KIAN KARIMI
A PASSION FOR SCIENCE AND SURGERY

Pg 09

DR KYLE R. SONG. MD
GIVING NATURE A HAND

Pg 15

MATTHEW DAVID HURTADO

FROM BANKRUPT TO MULTI MILLION $$ IN SALES. BRAIN-HACKING WITH RNA-DROPS SUPPLEMENTS

Pg 35

DR OSCAR RAMIREZ
BEAUTY IS BONE DEEP

Pg 21

ERIC BAILEY
FROM THE HOOD TO HOLLYWOOD

Pg 43

RAJA NALLURI
MAGIC WANDS

Pg 55

DR NATHANIEL PODILSKY
YOUR SMILE DESIGNER

Pg 29

DR. JOSEPH MINA ATALLA
SPECTACULAR SMILE

Pg 47

5 WAYS
TO STAY MOTIVATED

Pg 61

VERONICA GREY
LIVING LIFE WITH A PURPOSE

Pg 39

CAMIE J. CARPENTER
HOLLYWOOD TALENT MAKER

Pg 51

21 TIPS
TO BECOME THE MOST PRODUCTIVE PERSON YOU KNOW

Pg 63

JOHN ELLSWORTH

PROMOTING SPORTS
AND MENTAL TOUGHNESS

"I've always had a passion for helping others and an even higher level of passion for helping athletes perform better," says John Ellsworth, who for the last 16 years has been a sports psychology mental game coach for athletes. According to Ellsworth, licensed therapists, can work with individuals, and athletes from a clinical perspective. Educated and trained individuals in sports psychology, can work as mental game coaches and focus working with athletes primarily from a performance perspective, which has always been John's approach.

John states, "I'll get a call from a parent, an agent, or a professional athlete. The athlete, for whatever reason, is struggling to perform. They may be very good technically, but they aren't performing up to their expectations and desires. So what we try to do is help the athlete figure out why their performance isn't as good as they want it to be and then put together a plan to help them achieve their performance goals."

Ellsworth was looking for a career change away from the technology industry in the early 90's. He wanted to get back to a much earlier career in teaching and coaching so he decided to go back to school and get an advanced degree in psychology. His early training was in clinical family psychology and counseling, and later moved into sports psychology. While he started his career working only with families and children, he soon got referrals to work with athletes which allowed him to incorporate his life-long love of sports and coaching.

He continues to work with athletes of all ages, and skill levels, including professionals in the NFL, MLB, Professional Golf, as well as USA Track and Field that may perform well technically, but they have difficulties with practice situations, or challenges with self-confidence, focus or performance anxiety. Even when athletes possess a bunker crop of skill, they also need a strong mental game to increase their chances of winning.

Sports psychology can help athletes battle through a variety of performance challenges and to develop a much stronger sense of confidence, focus, and trust in their ability to perform at a higher level. Enhancing an athlete's ability to focus more in the present and less in the past or to not worry about the final score at the beginning of the game is a very important skill to possess. Having the mental toughness to not get overwhelmed in critical crunch time performance situations can make a big difference. Focusing on only one point at a time, or one game at a time, will keep them from getting overwhelmed. The biggest difference in their level of performance is related to their level of confidence and composure in pressure situations.

"Perfectionism is another significant problem that many young athletes in middle school, and high school struggle with." "The illusion of attaining perfection is also prevalent in sports that need a high level of technical mastery, like gymnastics, figure skating and golf," says Ellsworth. The difference between first and second place in these kinds of sports, can be very minor. Performing well for friends, parents, and up to the expectations of others, can drive the need to over practice, but also to over-perform.

Dedication, focus, and putting in the time, as well as wanting to achieve technical mastery, are all excellent pursuits, but trying to be too perfect also has a downside because athletes often overlook their best qualities.

"Generally speaking, perfectionism comes from an athlete over-demanding a high level of performance from himself, but their desired level of performance may not match up with their current skill level. They try and try, but their skill set doesn't match up with their performance demands. As a result they miss seeing how well they are actually doing in the present."

Ellsworth also talks about the concept of mental toughness, which he defines as, **"being in a stressful situation, and having the ability to dig deep within themselves and work through the challenges."** By developing self-discipline and a better mental game mindset, athletes can learn to overcome and recover from whatever challenges occur during a game, and to improve their overall performance.

"Not being able to perform a particular movement or skill could be the result of a number of things", says Ellsworth. One of them is fear, or an athlete might not have enough experience to build the necessary confidence.

They also may have experienced failure in the past, or they might be experiencing an over-demanding coach or feeling a parent's emotions rather than focusing on developing the necessary steps and skills.

"...being in a stressful situation, but the athlete has the ability to dig deep within themselves to be able to work themselves through their difficulties..."

Not every child is going to be a professional athlete, but intense pressure can definitely backfire, preventing them from enjoying themselves, or causing them to drop out of sports entirely. From his work with children and families, Ellsworth explains how parents see their children in relation to sports, and the kind of support the athlete receives as they pursue their sport has a large influence on self-esteem development. Ellsworth says, "As much as 40 to 50 percent of the challenges that he sees with middle school and high school athletes, and sometimes even college athletes, has a lot to do with the pressure they feel from others. When athletes are young, everyone, including parents, need to be part of a support team that is focused on creating positive and enjoyable experiences.

An athlete's support team should be driven by a common set of principles and values focused on guiding the athlete in the direction they want to go. That is the purpose of working on a vision statement with someone like a mental game coach. Such vision building involves helping the athlete to see clearly his goals for the season or distant future, and how to get there. Everyone wants to win, but from a support team perspective everyone needs to understand the athlete's desires and work together to help them achieve their goals and enjoy the process.

"I find that it is extremely important for an athlete and his support team to have an idea of what it is they are trying to accomplish. What is the vision the athlete sees for themselves and not what the parents want for the athlete? It's not just about wanting to be a better baseball player, a better football player, or a better tennis player. It's more about the helping to lay out an overall vision of where they want to be a year or two years from now," John Ellsworth.

Ellsworth also points to the rising cost of participating in sports as a challenge for many families because they just can't afford it, and that can definitely add to the pressure. To combat that, four years ago, John started a nonprofit foundation called the Protex Sports Foundation whose mission is focused on providing funding for disadvantaged and financially-challenged families for training, camps, and to keep kids active in sports.

(http://protexsportsfoundation.org/).

Sponsors can donate through the website and parents can also visit the website to apply for a grant. Once a year, usually in the spring, the Foundation staff reviews grant applications, selecting as many as they can so these families and their athletes can achieve their dreams. Even if they don't become professionals in their chosen sport, the lessons can last a lifetime, and everyone should have that opportunity.

For further information or to inquire about **Sports Psychology services from Protex Sports and John Ellsworth**, please go to:

www.protexsports.com
or call 1-800-608-1120

DR. KIAN KARIMI

A passion for Science and Surgery

"I knew early on that the sciences were my passion. I used to follow my father when he would go on hospital rounds or see patients with him in his clinic. I witnessed how unique and powerful the doctor – patient relationship was, and I knew then, at 5 years old, that I wanted to be a doctor," Kian Karimi MD, FACS.

As a double-board certified facial plastic surgeon and a head and neck surgeon, as well as the Medical Director of both Rejuva Medical Aesthetics and CosmoFrance Inc., Dr. Kian Karimi (drkian.com) is practically born for a white coat. He also serves as one of the team plastic surgeons for the Los Angeles Kings Hockey organization. From childhood he was exposed to a science based family, with guidance from a father who is a physican and a mother who is a professor of microbiology and immunology.

It was no surprise that early in medical school, he decided to become a surgeon. He says he fell in love with the anatomy of the head and neck because of the intricacies and detail involved, which evolved into an interest in facial plastic surgery. He states, **"I am blessed to be in a position where I can help people feel better about themselves and to treat medical issues, as well to heal both the inside and the outside."**

Dr. Kian was also happy to share how he and his partner, Dr. Chester Griffiths MD, founded Rejuva Medical Aesthetics (rejuvamedical.org) in Los Angeles this year, which is a state-of-the art, minimally invasive, medical aesthetic center.

"We have beautiful, new facilities with the latest advances in aesthetic medicine to allow our patients to maintain a beautiful, natural appearance."

At the same time, Dr. Kian accented the facility's calming decor with a beautiful view of the mountains that feels more like a spa than a medical office.

Under the guidance of Dr. Kian, Rejuva offers multiple services from medical grade skin care, neuromodulator treatments (e.g. Botox, Xeomin, Dysport), Hydrafacials, photofacial IPL treatments, microneedling, and platelet rich plasma. In the non-surgical realm, his practice is known across the country for their bruiseless filler techniques that uses a smooth tip microcannula to deliver filler, rather than a traditional needle on the face and body. People often fly in specifically for the procedure, and their expertise was also featured on EXTRA TV and CBS 'The Doctors', earlier this year.

"A successful surgeon is a lifelong student — we have to continue to study, question what we do and why, and constantly stay on top of the latest techniques and technologies. As surgeons, we have a unique role to provide both medical and surgical solutions to problems," Kian Karimi MD, FACS.

Facial fat transfers and non-surgical neck tightening with ThermiTight and Kybella fat dissolving injections are also popular procedures. For dramatic improvements of the skin, laser resurfacing is the main modality including treatments with a new HALO hybrid laser which delivers full resurfacing results without the downtime. Their newest service is lifting with PDO threads (Novathreads™), which allow them to lift the midface and lower one-third of the face right in the office, an area where fillers are not always successful on their own. They are one of the first places to offer the service in the United States, although dissolvable threads are already quite popular in Asia and Europe, as a non-surgical adjunct to fillers with little or no down-time.

Dr. Kian also advises his patients to live well by exercising and eating properly. He says, **"I spend extra time with my patients, especially new patients, to find out their motivations, goals, and expectations. This extra effort allows me to not only consistently enhance my patients' appearance, but also to enhance their lives."**

Dr. Kian emphasized the partnership between a patient's health and appearance with their doctors or surgeons when mapping what they want to achieve and setting timelines for how to maintain excellent health and a beautiful, refreshed appearance. He underscores healthy habits and to remove toxins from our lives to maximize our aesthetics and to feel good about ourselves, inside and out. He wants patients to, **"take care of themselves and perform aesthetic enhancements conscientiously."**

On a day-to-day basis though, Dr. Kian recommends a good sunscreen and moisturizer to protect the skin from drying out and from UV damage, which he explains is one of the greatest factors that will age us. He also recommends a procedure called "ForeverYoung BBL," which is a special kind of photofacial that actually slows down the aging genes of the skin, as proven by a study at Stanford University. By performing the procedure only three times a year, patients get better quality skin with less pigment issues, less fine lines, and overall more resilient skin years later than when they started having the procedures performed..

Dr. Kian's office also offers a wide variety of surgical procedures, such as rhinoplasty, revision rhinoplasty, face and neck lifts, neck liposuction, endoscopic browlifts, otoplasty(the correction of protruding ears), and the reconstruction of facial trauma and skin cancer defects. Dr. Kian proudly says that, **"Surgically, we are best known for our natural and beautiful rhinoplasty results — as facial plastic surgeons, this is really our main forte. Face and necklifting are also a particular strength of ours as well."** Chin and facial implants and surgery of the upper and lower eyelid are common too, along with corrective work to fix or improve on previously performed procedures that did not produce the desired outcome.

When it comes to his own health and happiness, Dr. Kian practices what he preaches and clearly points to the importance of a good work-life balance in his busy life. He runs and works out with a personal trainer at least twice a week, -eats well, and strongly believes in getting good quality sleep. He also said, "I enjoy spending time with my supportive wife who is also a busy physician – we like to get away and travel, when we can, to maximize our time together."

Dr. Kian sees a bright and exciting future for the constantly changing fields of medicine, science and surgery, now that we have decoded the human genetic sequence. He credits the vast amounts of information about health and disease are being found, adding that, "Stem cell therapies hold tremendous promise, in both therapeutic and aesthetic medicine. In plastic surgery, the most exciting promises of these technologies are to create your own tissues just from taking a few of your stem cells and directing these cells to turn into whatever tissue graft or filler you want." Dr. Kian is also responsible for teaching future surgeons at UCLA, and he has medical students and resident physicians rotate at his office.

"We teach future surgeons and physicians that patient-centered care is the key. We owe it to our patients to treat them with respect, ethically recommend options for aesthetic and therapeutic issues, and to stay on top of our field, by constantly researching, reading, and conferring with colleagues." Kian Karimi MD, FACS.

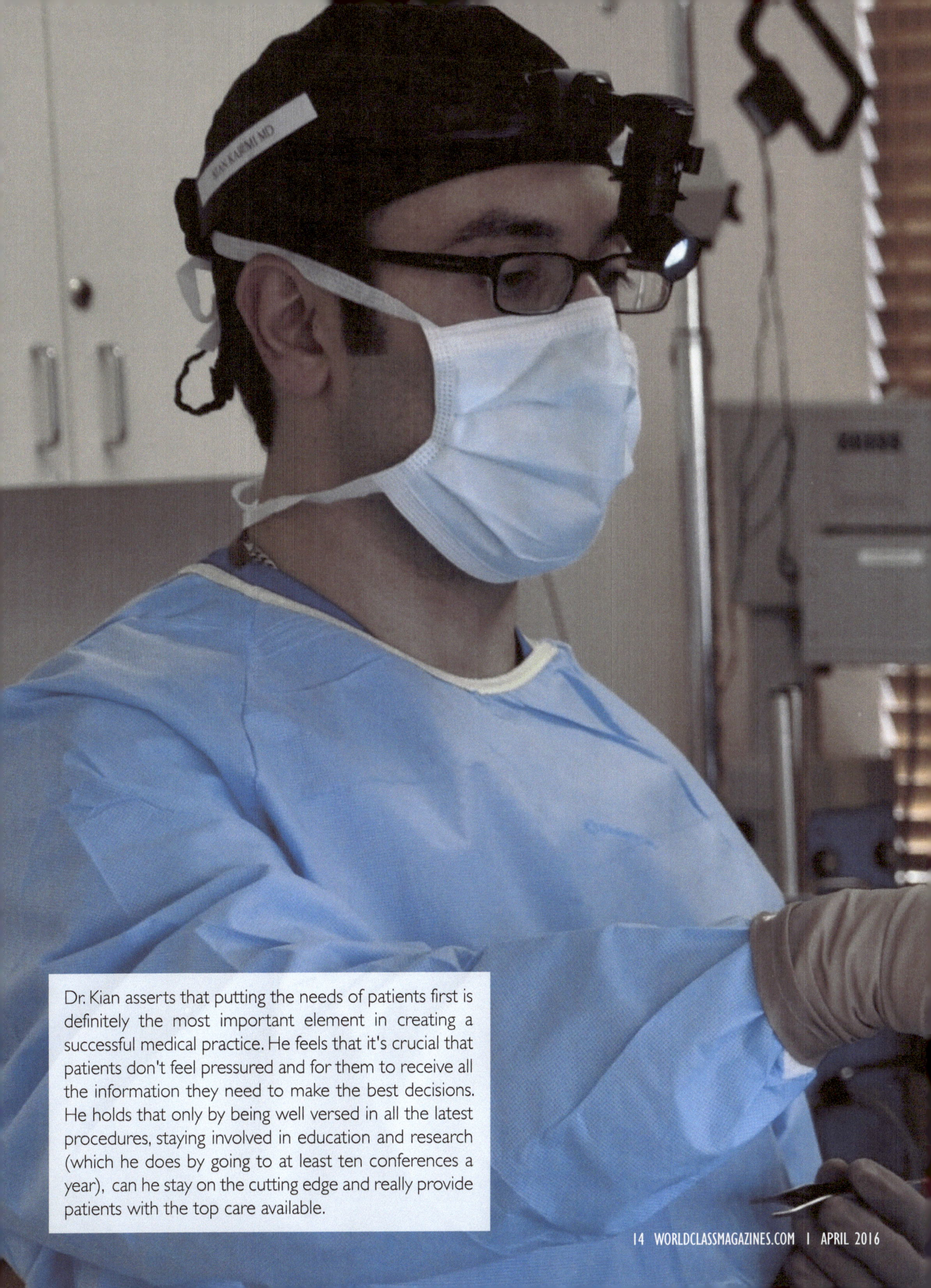

Dr. Kian asserts that putting the needs of patients first is definitely the most important element in creating a successful medical practice. He feels that it's crucial that patients don't feel pressured and for them to receive all the information they need to make the best decisions. He holds that only by being well versed in all the latest procedures, staying involved in education and research (which he does by going to at least ten conferences a year), can he stay on the cutting edge and really provide patients with the top care available.

We understand that plastic surgery is an incredibly personal experience. You should trust and feel comfortable with your surgeon and their team.

DR. KYLE R. SONG, MD
Giving Nature a Hand

Our relationship with our bodies is deeply personal, so it's important to find a plastic surgeon that understands the value of personalized attention with supportive and compassionate care.

Dr. Kyle Song (http://www.kylesongmd.com) is an Orange County leader for both plastic and reconstructive surgeries, offering cosmetic procedures for the face, body and breast, as well as skin care. Patient satisfaction is the driving force behind his business at Song Plastic Surgery in Irvine, CA, pushing him to deliver long-lasting, natural results.

Dr. Song's passion for his work has been recognized in his presentations at regional, national and international venues, and even early in his career he has been awarded accordingly, including the Francis W. Noel award for scholarly activity during residency, and as runner-up for the resident research competition at the California Society of Plastic Surgeons annual meeting in 2011. Because Dr. Song is himself a younger doctor, he often attracts a younger clientele, since his education is more recent, and he fully understands what they are looking for.

Dieting and exercise can only do so much to fight nature. Dr. Song specializes and is known for the "Mommy Makeover" procedure – a combination of breast and tummy surgery to reverse the anatomical and physiological changes that come with age, pregnancy and nursing. Breast augmentation, itself, has become increasingly popular. In fact, there were almost 300,000 breast augmentation cases in 2011, in the United States, which moved it to the top of the charts for plastic surgery procedures across the country.

In 2015, Dr. Song was named a "Top Doctor" for breast augmentation by Realself.com, a patient-driven forum on all matters plastic surgery.

There are various breast implant types and sizes including subtle, small implants to improve shape and symmetry. Actually, when it comes to saline and silicone implants, there are literally thousands of possible combinations of implants, incision locations, and implant placement, so consultation with a knowledgeable and compassionate doctor is crucial for patients to make the best decision. Dr. Song also uses an augmented reality software to visualize post-operative results in real-time, which improves patient-physician communication, and by demonstrating a realistic expectation after surgery, it helps ease the fear of the unknown.

Motherhood definitely brings with it a multitude of changes both psychological and physical, but it's important for women to think about themselves too, so they can be at their best as caregivers. Weight reduction and body contouring procedures are a crucial part of Dr. Song's services, for women at any life stage, including tummy tucks and liposuction, as well as lifts of the butt, breasts, thighs, arms and the whole body.

A "Mommy Makeover" combines reshaping of the breasts with tummy tuck surgery and liposuction to revitalize the entre body. Since each woman's body is different, there is no one-size-fits-all surgery solution, but stretched abdominal muscles, a sagging or protruding belly, stretch marks, love handles, and loss of breast tissue can all be addressed.

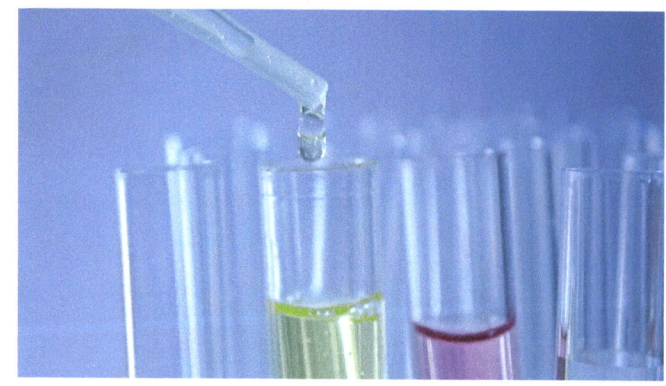

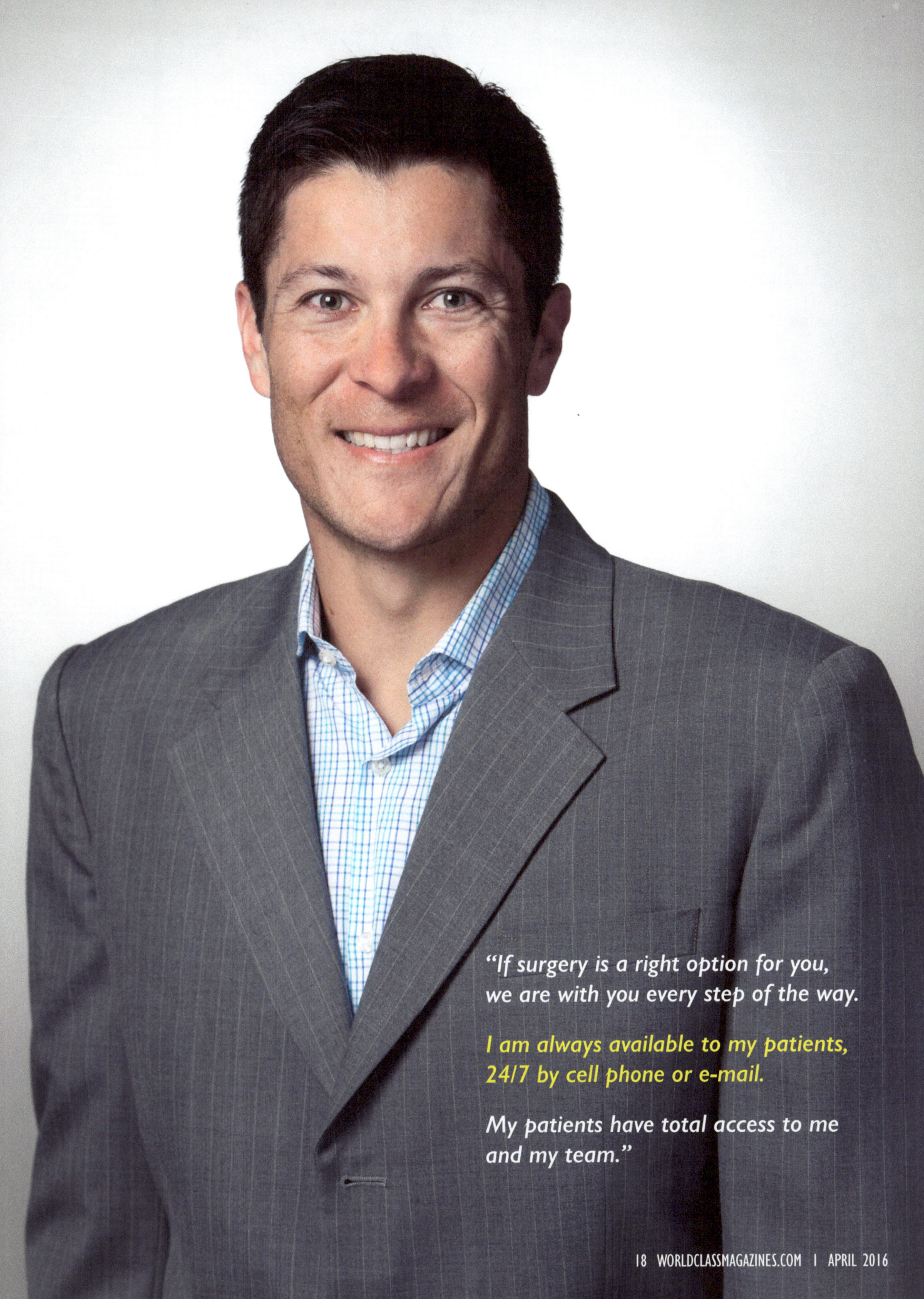

A breast lift procedure can be combined with the augmentation to deal with sagging, but breast reductions are also growing in popularity for men too, since up to 60 percent of them exhibit some degree of gynecomastia. This over-development of male breast tissue can be caused by inherited genetic traits or obesity, as well as by metabolic disorders and certain medications or drugs, such as steroids and marijuana.

We tend to think of the front of our bodies more often, but it's not the only thing to consider when it comes to a woman's shape and what makes it attractive, although of course that is a very individual thing too. Dr. Song performs Brazilian Butt Lifts to deal with sagging skin and lots of volume there as well, which can be especially pronounced after weight loss. Fat can be harvested during a tummy tuck or buttocks lift and deposited to the upper part of the butt for a firmer more attractive shape.

A patient's confidence and identity are often deeply connected to how attractive they think they look. Breast lifts, reductions, augmentation and body surgery can bring back a more positive body-image or give them to figure that they've always dreamed of. This is, of course, even more important when it comes to breast reconstruction for women who are missing part or all of a breast because of cancer, trauma or genetics.

Conducting clinical research is another of Dr. Song's interests, **and he has been published in several peer-reviewed periodicals. His contributions to plastic surgery have been as extensive as his travels, as he has brought reconstructive surgical services to impoverished children around the world, such as cleft lip and cleft palate repair in Egypt and reconstructive surgery to the victims of the Hermosillo Daycare fire in Tijuana, Mexico.**

If there's a particular part of your body that you find yourself concerned about, and you're not totally happy with, Dr. Song can help you do something about it, be that a cosmetic, plastic surgery, or a noninvasive med-spa procedure. Sometimes, we have to give nature a hand because looking are best at any age is something that all men and women want, so they can feel confident and great about themselves.

To make an appointment, contact Dr. Song's office:
OFFICE 949 701 4454
www.kylesongmd.com

DR. OSCAR RAMIREZ

BEAUTY is BONE DEEP

"The common view is that beauty is skin deep, but in my view beauty is more than that. From a physical point of view, beauty is down to the bone, especially on the face. A good facial structure will determine if a face is beautiful or not," Dr. Oscar Ramirez.

Skeletal structure provides lift, support, angles and contour relief to make faces more attractive and younger looking, according to Dr. Oscar Ramirez. **(http://www.ramirezmd.com/).**

With that in mind, he designed more than ten different facial implants and the RZ Mandibular Matrix System, as well as a complete line of EndoFacelift™ instruments. **These instruments and implants were critical to facilitate the many surgical procedures that Dr Ramirez has invented to beautify and rejuvenate the face.**

His porous, polyethylene implants have special channels that allow the tissue and blood vessels to grow right into them, allowing them to actually become a part of the face's structure. This means that they require very exacting techniques and dexterity to attach them to the bone, but they are a big improvement on common silicone implants, which tend to erode the bone and move over time.

Recent studies show that facial bones become smaller and thinner with aging, degrading over time, as shown by three dimensional CAT scans. This loss of bone structure, however, can be safely and easily replaced with implants for rejuvenation and beautification. They can then provide a foundation for working with the soft tissues of the face, the fat layer, the muscles and the skin. Bone grafts from the hips or other areas can also be used, but that is a major and much more risky surgery, which is usually reserved for patients with congenital anomalies.

Dr. Ramirez's RZ Mandibular Matrix System restructures and redefines the whole lower jaw, face, chin and neck with multiple implants for people who have lost bone mass because they no longer have teeth or for facial enhancement. For example, Dr. Ramirez says that a strong chin and jaw can give a face more authority or masculinity. Over time, women have also moved away from softer facial features to have more structure too. Implants can be placed on any part of the face, such as the cheeks, the lower and upper orbits, or the temples.

"If you peruse any glamour magazine, you can see that the most beautiful models have strong skeletal support in their faces. They have nice cheekbones. They have a good angle on the mandible and good definition in the neck and the chin," Dr. Oscar Ramirez.

Face lifts simply rely on stretching and pulling, which results in tight, shiny skin around the ears and lateral cheeks with loose skin in the center of the face. Dr. Ramirez, however, specializes in facial, endoscopic rejuvenation and beautification, which addresses the central oval of the face, lifts in a more vertical direction, against gravity, with much smaller incisions. This elevates the brow and rejuvenates the mid-face, jaw line, chin and neck, without removing any skin for many patients, creating a more attractive, oval shape.

Dr. Ramirez is often called on to fix the mistakes of others too. He says that many surgeons shy away from doing such secondary surgeries because it's always a challenge to repair someone else's work. Scarring and distortion make it more difficult, so it can never be completely perfect. Dr. Ramirez points to rhinoplasty, in particular, as the most difficult procedure in plastic surgery because it involves bone, cartilage, different skin thicknesses and the actual airway of the nose, which needs to remain fully functional.

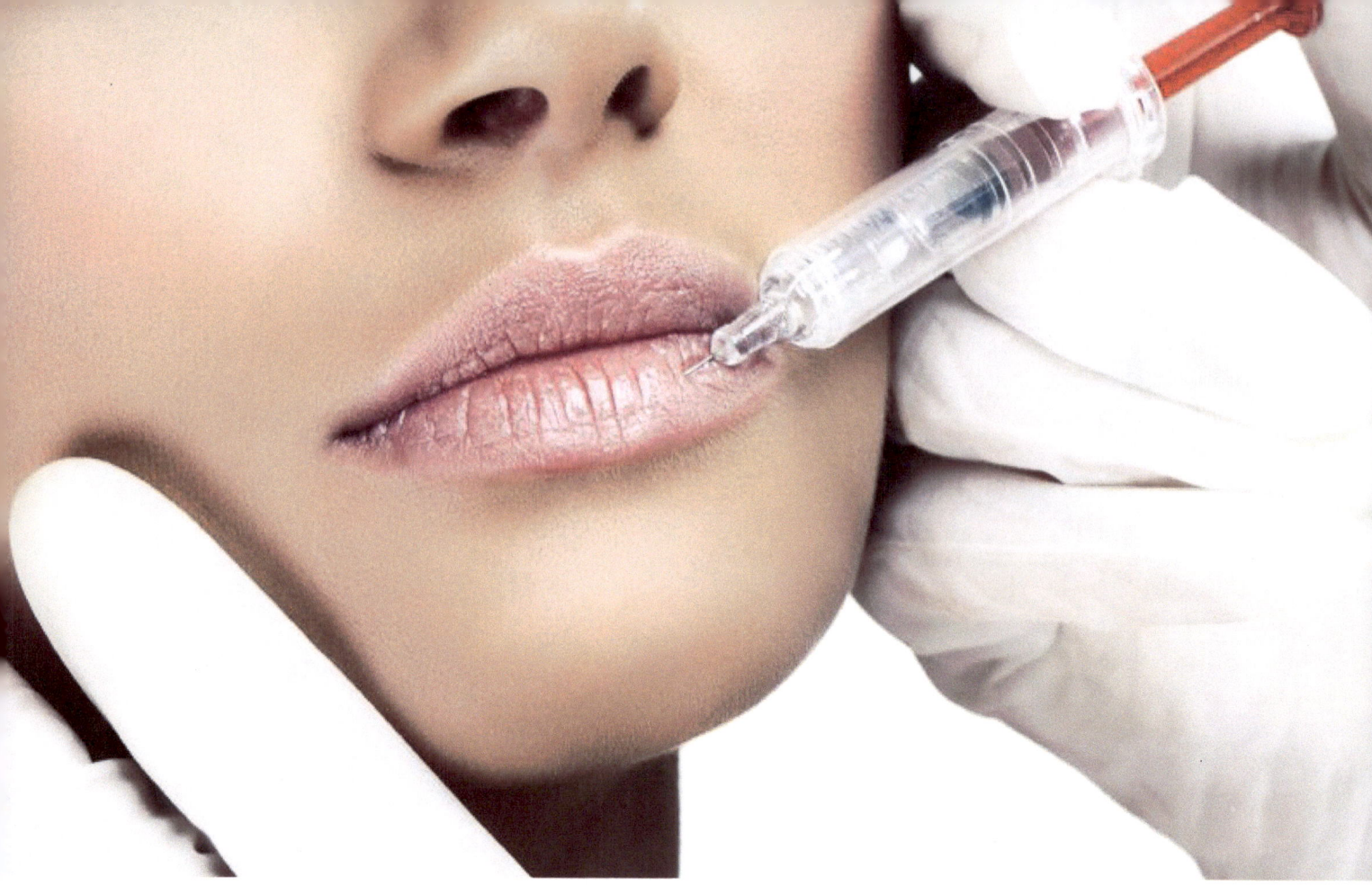

Complications can result from either aesthetics or functionality. Often, there can be issues with both. Additional materials and cartilage are required because all areas of the nose need special support to prevent collapse in the long-term when removing cartilage to make a nose smaller.

"When you do a rhinoplasty, you have to provide enough support, even to add extra support, to the new nose. And, that nose will look better at the beginning and ten years later," Dr. Oscar Ramirez.

Body contouring is even more popular than facial surgeries, in Dr. Ramirez's practice, including liposuction, breast augmentation and reduction, and work on the thighs or arms. Liposuction can even be done under local anesthesia right in his office, while patients are awake and only slightly sedated with minimal blood loss. Younger patients have more elasticity, so the skin on the abdomen and thighs contract better than in older patients who are over 40, or who have had children. Those patients may also require abdominoplasty or removal skin and stretch marks.

Dr. Ramirez explains that, indeed, there's an exact science to beauty through what is called the golden ratio also called divine proportions. This describes certain mathematical proportions, which have been known since antiquity. Recently, this has also been popularized in books like "The DaVinci Code," but it can also be used to create beautiful, well-balanced faces. This ratio was associated with the art of DaVinci and attributed to Fibonacci but the initial description was done by Euclid in "Elements" by 300 B.C. Many other mathematicians and artists have intuitively used it because our brains seem to be hardwired to prefer objects with this special ratio.

"The golden ratio exists in beautiful objects in nature, in animals, and plants, and obviously, in different parts of the body. It happens that this mathematical relationship is 1.618 or if you put it in simplistic terms, it is about 2/3 to 1/3. Among the different segments of the face, for example, a beautiful person is somebody who has 1/3 on each of the segments of the face: on the upper, middle and lower face." Dr. Oscar Ramirez.

Dr. Ramirez is an international speaker on advanced plastic surgery techniques who has authored over one hundred fifty articles, as well as several textbooks on aesthetic surgery and endoscopic surgical techniques. He was also named one of 2,000 Outstanding Scientists in the 21st Century by the International Biographical Centre in Cambridge, England, for his contributions in plastic and reconstruction surgery. His more than 30 years of experience put him at the top of his field, so in this case, beauty is not just in the eye of the beholder, its foundation is rock-solid.

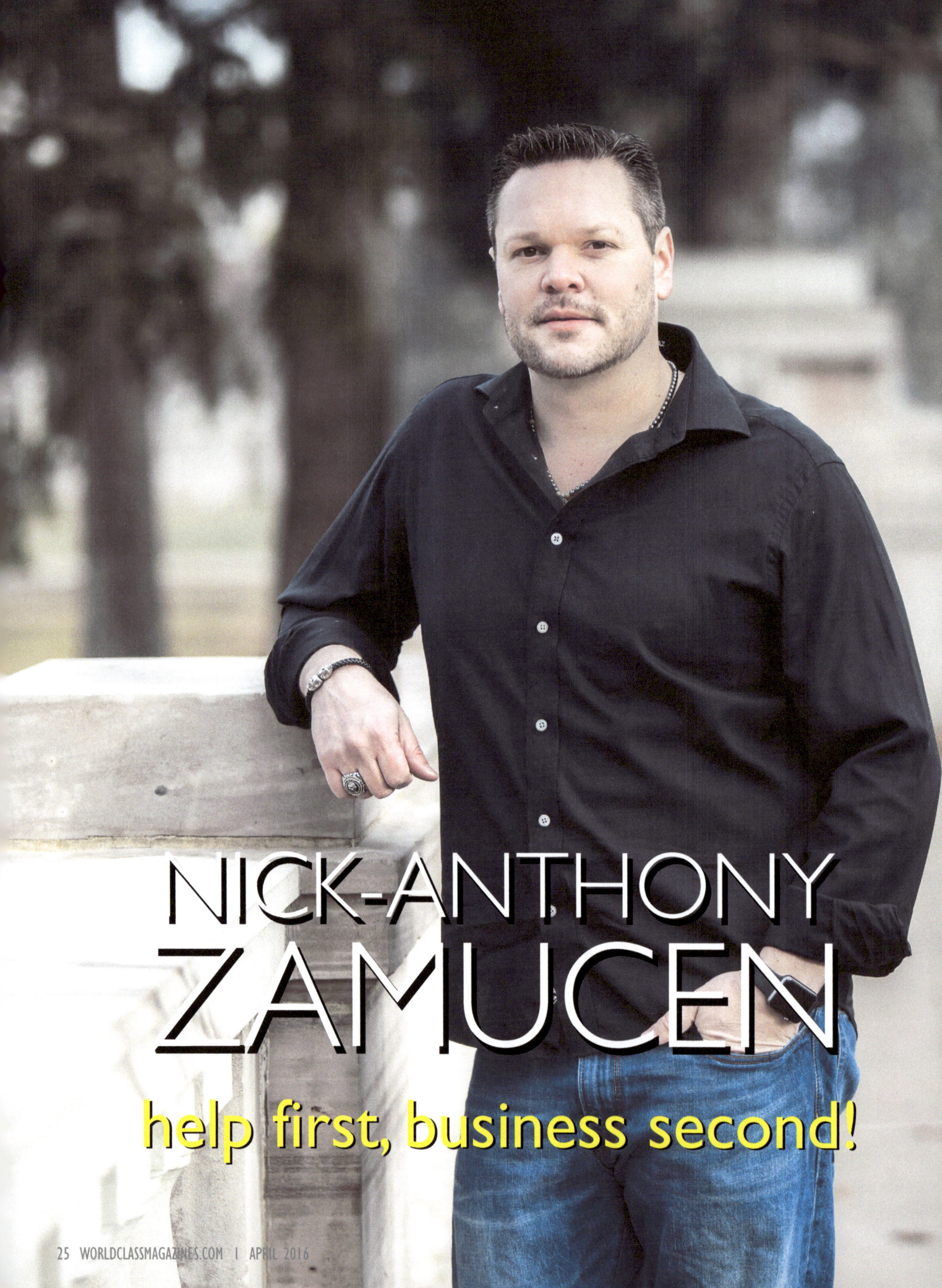

Regardless of the number of times you hear Nick-Anthony Zamucen's success story, it never gets boring. His success story is not only timeless, it's rare. Hardly do we come across a franchising business which has 100% success rate. Nick-Anthony's company, Bio-One Inc is one of those rare ones. Bio-One has been around for over twenty years but only began franchising four years ago. It has not had a franchise that has not broken even within eight months. In most business models, breaking even within the first two to three years is considered pretty impressive. What Nick-Anthony's company has achieved is phenomenal.

The story of how Nick-Anthony began his company is just as fascinating as the incredible success story the company has become. About two decades ago during a church service, the minister told the congregation to go check on one of the church members whose husband had committed suicide. She was not in the service and the pastor knew she needed to be comforted. Nick-Anthony was a church member at that church in southern Georgia. He and a few other church members decided to visit the woman and see how she was doing. They found her seated on the couch. She had not moved from the couch for four days. She pointed them to the back of the door and told them that the police had told her to clean that herself. They did not know what she was talking about. They checked the back of the door that led to the bedroom.

The bedroom was a mess. Blood was everywhere. It was quite clear to them at this stage that her husband had shot himself to death. Some of her fellow church members took her to lunch. The others, including Nick-Anthony, were left cleaning up the mess. Nick-Anthony says back then, they did several things wrong as they cleaned up, but all they wanted to do was to help. He says this is why one of the core beliefs of his company is helping first and doing the business second.

After the cleanup, they discussed the matter and wondered how people across the country deal with such traumatic events. Nick-Anthony wondered how many other cases similar to this were happening in the United States. Then the idea was born. Back then there were no bio companies.

"What if we started a crime scene cleanup company and could actually help people in this time of need?"

Nick-Anthony believes that you have to work every day as if you are going to lose your job; like that is your last to make a difference. This is what he teaches Bio-One franchisees. He believes this is the secret to Bio-One's incredible success.

For Bio-One, business is everywhere. Nick-Anthony says when they are deciding where to put up a franchise they look purely at the population. He says every year in a population of a million people, there is going to be around 73 suicides, around 24 homicides, a little over 17,000 domestic violence cases and over 30,000 aggravated assaults. These are the numbers they use to determine how much work they are likely to find there.

Bio-One franchising clients come from all over the board; from the military, ex-law enforcement and even ex-firemen just to mention a few. In fact, one of Nick-Anthony's most successful stories was a stay home mom whose kid had left for college and now she wanted to use her time contributing positively as a member of her society. **Nick-Anthony says anyone can succeed franchising this business as long as he has the ability to want to go out and become a productive member of society and have a passion for making a difference in their community every day.**

Most people who become Bio-One franchisees are usually people who are already looking for a franchising business. Because of the nature of the business, it is not a business that families can talk about around the dinner table. Many who join Bio-One get to learn about it online or through a broker. A good number of others decide to join the business because they have gone through a traumatizing experience that they wish no one would have to go through.

Nick-Anthony does not require a person to have had experience in business or bio-recovery. He uses whatever life experiences they have to mold them into a prosperous entrepreneur. Nick-Anthony believes his gift is his ability to find the best in someone and multiply that more than they ever thought was possible.

"Give me the person as a piece of clay and I will make them an entrepreneur sculpture," says Nick-Anthony, **"It's amazing to take somebody who came from the corporate world that has never been an entrepreneur and to see them make their first million dollars and realize that it actually does still happen."**

Nick-Anthony intimates that most of Bio-One franchises end up hiring people in law enforcement or former law enforcement, firemen or emergency medical technicians (EMTs). This is because these people will, more often than not, have been needle-stick and blood borne pathogen certified. They will also have been on crime and traumatizing scenes before and so will not be shocked by what they will see in the field.

Bio-One is preparing to launch internationally. It will be the first crime and trauma scene cleaning company to ever go international. Nick-Anthony says they are very excited by the prospect of going into Canada, United Kingdom, Spain, France and the Netherlands.

To those people who are still struggling with the decision of going into this industry: "This is an industry that is like no other. It's a recession-proof industry. It's not going anywhere," Nick-Anthony says, "Unfortunately, people do pass away. People do hurt each other and hurt themselves. And it's not gonna stop regardless of the economy – so it is not economy-driven."

"And as of right now, we still have never had a franchise fail underneath the Bio-One flag. So we are at 100% success rate. We're about as perfect as you get."

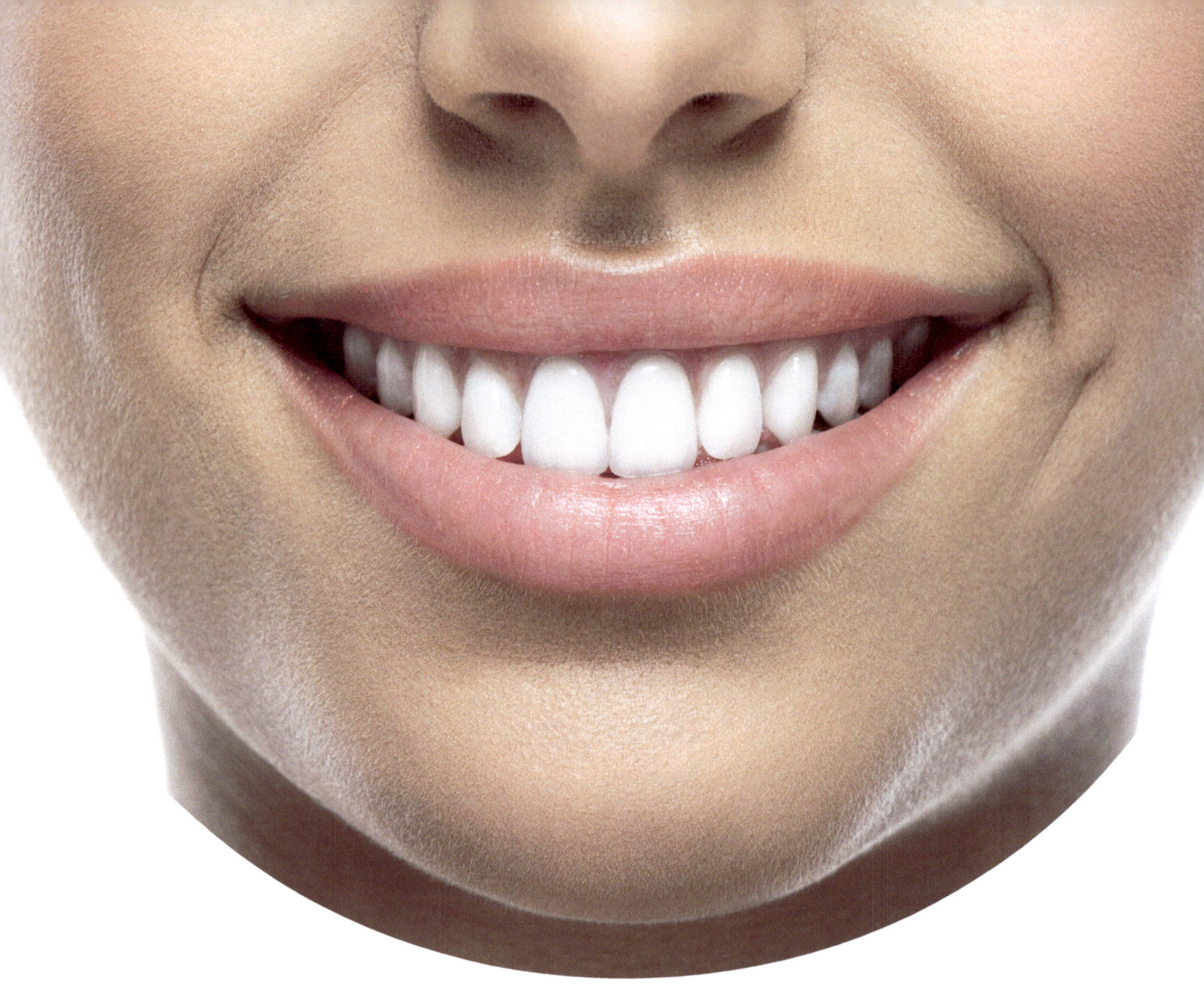

DR. NATHANIEL PODILSKY
your smile designer

there is nothing more rewarding for a dentist than to give a patient a new smile and essentially change the person's life.

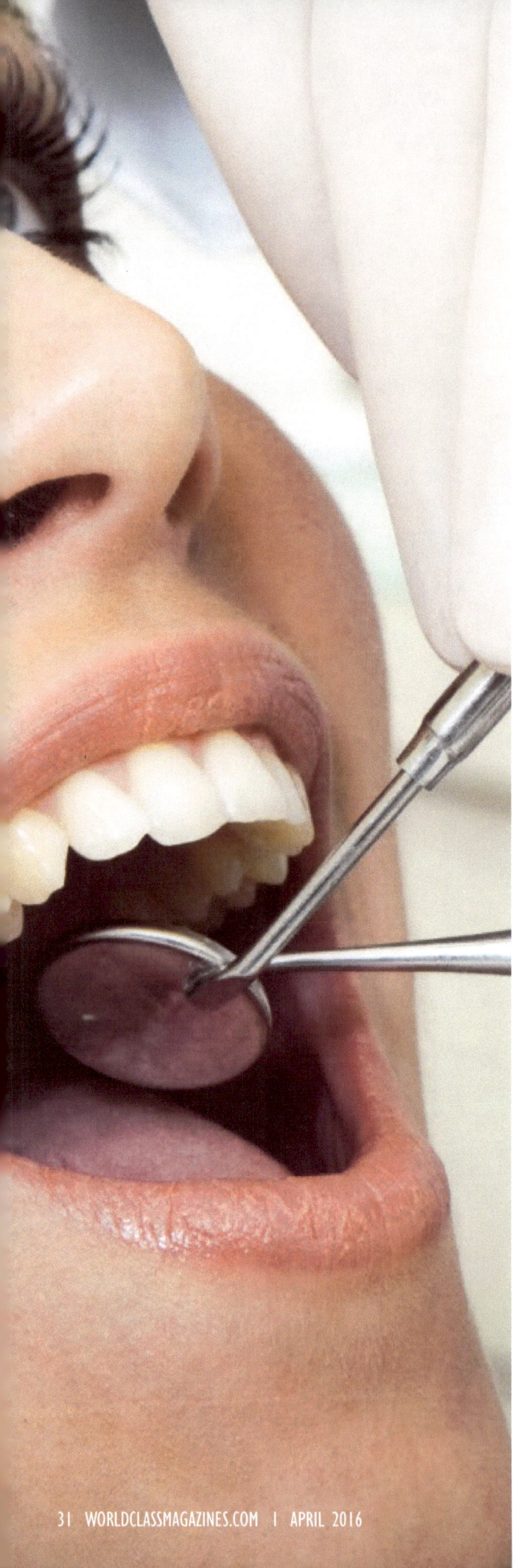

For the last 34 years, Dr. Nathaniel Podilsky has served the people of Edmonton, Alberta with General, Cosmetic and Implant Dentistry. His practice focuses on implants, smile design, tooth replacement and orthodontic treatment. He graduated from the University of Saskatchewan in 1982 and went ahead to open his general dental practice in the "ice district" of downtown Edmonton, Canada.

Dr Podilsky's Smile Design program involves both the white esthetics (teeth) and the pink esthetics (gums). It is focused on gum architecture, proportion and relation of the teeth to one another, color and shape of the teeth and the length of the teeth. Before a dentist can put Porcelain veneers into a person's mouth, there will be a number of things he has to consider to ensure you get that smile you are yearning for. Dr Podilsky says the process usually takes anywhere from four to six weeks depending on the patient's time, his time and the lab's time. During this time, he schedules multiple appointments to review the patient's expectations, choose the best smile design for the patient from a "smile" catalog, decide how many teeth the patient should show and their color and review the patient's teeth in relation to their face and smile.

Dr Nathaniel Podilsky says while this process is quite complex, there is nothing more rewarding for a dentist than to give a patient a new smile and essentially change the person's life. And he enjoys every minute of it.

Once the patients have undergone a restorative smile transformation "they (patients) tend to no longer hide their smile, they tend to smile more often, they tend to show more self-confidence, and so it changes their lives," Dr Podilsky says.

When constructing Porcelain veneers, Dr Podilsky considers the positioning of the teeth to determine how to prepare the tooth. He then takes the patient through a smile catalog and discusses their expectations. After that, impressions of the patient's teeth are taken; the impressions are then made into models. The models are used to make a wax up to determine what the teeth are going to look like, how long they will be and their relationship to one another. This takes around 10 days. After this, the patient is required to go in for a fairly lengthy appointment where the doctor determines how many teeth they should have prepared, usually eight teeth on the upper jaw. Sometimes porcelain veneers are placed on the bottom front teeth if they show when a person smiles or speaks.

From the "wax up", a guide is used to form temporaries which are then placed on the patient. The doctor uses the temporaries to determine what the smile will look like and how they will function with the patient's current bite. Dr Podilsky calls this "test-driving the smile". At this stage, he discusses with his patient their preferred color of teeth. As a general rule, teeth are never one shade. They are made in multiple shades, usually lighter towards the biting surface of the tooth with some translucency and darker towards the gum line.

Once the patient has decided on the shades preferred, the dental impressions are sent to the lab for fabrication. Fabrication of porcelain veneers takes between 10 days to two weeks. The patient returns for another appointment during which the temporaries are removed and the doctor fits the veneers and checks them in natural light and in the dental operatory. Once Dr Podilsky counterchecks everything and gives it a green light, he bonds the Porcelain veneers on to the natural dentition and polishes them. The patient goes in for one more appointment where the doctor checks the occlusion (bite) as well as tissue healing around the veneers.

Dr Podilsky recommends people who have had Porcelain veneers fitted to have a night guard fabricated. The night guard protects the veneers from teeth grinding while the person is sleeping. This is also known as bruxism and is often involuntary. For people who are actively involved in sports, Dr Podilsky recommends that they also get a custom sports guard fabricated. The sports guard protects the Porcelain veneers from damage during active contact sports. Dr Podilsky explains of one of his patient's veneers that are still in perfect condition over 12 years later even though the patient is very active in bob sledding. He says the secret to the Porcelain veneers' longevity is the use of a sports guard, a night guard, good home care and regular hygiene visits at the dentist.

"This lady, that was active in bob sledding, would crash every single day. She wore a sports guard throughout her bob sledding career. Her Porcelain veneers are still bonded on and that's at least 12 years old," commented Dr Podilsky.

Dr Nathaniel Podilsky also does full mouth reconstruction. This typically involves replacing missing teeth, replacing old crowns and closing gaps between the teeth. He says the majority of the time he tries to be very conservative. Porcelain Veneers are more conservative than full crowns since they require less tooth preparation. For that reason, whenever possible, Dr Podilsky prefers to construct veneers in the front rather than fit many crowns.

There are instances when Dr Podilsky might decide to fit crowns rather than veneers. These include replacing an old existing crown which has decay under it, if the tooth is weak because it has an existing root canal or if there is not enough enamel around the tooth for bonding because of acid erosion or wear. Dr Podilsky says the reason he prefers veneers to crowns is because today people are living longer; up to eighty and ninety years old. There is a good chance the veneers or crowns will need to be replaced over this time.

Most people who undergo these dental procedures become more confident and outgoing, they stop putting their hands over their mouths while talking and they smile more often. Getting a brand new smile may also improve in interpersonal relationships.

Dr Podilsky says, **"Smiling is one of the major factors when people look at other people and it's the first impression. The smile is one of the first things that most people will see other than the eyes. So it's crucial to have a very good smile."**

Dr Podilsky also emphasizes the importance of replacing missing teeth. All teeth are important in function and in the longevity of other teeth. According to Dr Podilsky, front and back teeth have functions which are unique to each of them. The front teeth cut the food and make sure that the back teeth don't touch when one functions or chews sideways and in a forward direction. So if you are missing the front teeth, the back teeth become worn out and become very flat. On the other hand, if you are missing the back teeth, the front teeth are forced to grind, a function they are not designed for. As a result, the front teeth start chipping, cracking and eventually break off. Ultimately you may lose the front teeth due to the stresses on them. Implants are a great alternative to tooth replacement if you are missing any teeth. By replacing the missing teeth you are preventing movement of the other teeth and you are protecting your natural teeth from wear and tear in normal everyday function.

According to Dr Podilsky, it is extremely important for a person to replace a tooth within the first year of losing a tooth. When you lose teeth, the bone around the area with the missing teeth begins to disappear or resorb away. The bone disappears in width, height and even quality throughout a person's life. This can never be fully replaced even with the new surgical techniques currently used in dentistry.

"It's very much like if you go to the gym and one arm gets exercised and the other one doesn't. The one arm that's not exercised the muscles become atrophic or very weak while the other arm becomes very muscular, very strong. Bone is the same way. Bones responds to and needs function." Natural teeth and dental implants provide for this function.

It is great news for patients that they can enhance and improve their smile at any age and in any condition. Dr Podilsky says there is no age limit when people can get veneers, crowns or even implants. His mother received implants at the age of 88. She is now 92 and eats better and functions better. Because of this, her overall general health is better.

To keep your teeth healthy, Dr Podilsky recommends that you watch your diet, employ proper nutritional practices and watch the amount of sugar you ingest daily. He also recommends using electric toothbrushes to brush your teeth. In fact, he says clinically they have been found to be a thousand times better than manual toothbrushes. Dr Podilsky also recommends regular visits to your dentist's office for teeth examinations and oral cancer examinations.

To get in touch with Dr Podilsky, you can visit their website at:
https://www.cosmeticdentistryedmonton.com
His practice is now open on alternate Saturdays in addition to weekdays (Monday to Friday).

"There are things you can do to activate the law of reciprocity to have things come to you..."

MATTHEW DAVID HURTADO

Everyone told him it was not possible, but Matthew David Hurtado went ahead to cure himself of Lyme disease using his mindset. Matthew was unreasonable. He consistently refused to align with what every medical doctor told him would be his fate. He opted for a mindset where Lyme disease would be unable to exist. He chose to be stubborn and changed his expectations even when it seemed like he was simply being hardheaded.

Today, Matthew Hurtado is completely cured of Lyme disease and is a successful businessman. His rise to success in business is the other incredible story of his life. In less than three years, he turned around his fortunes and moved from bankruptcy to making 7-figures. He is the CEO of Complete Ascentials and the author of Allow, an Amazon best-seller.

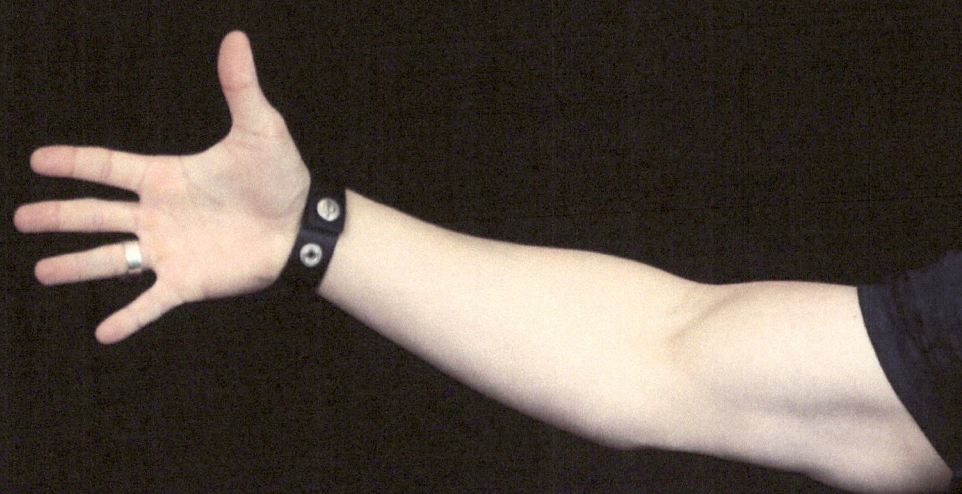

As Matthew struggled with the so-called incurable disease, his businesses suffered. At that moment, all he could think about was the probability that he was going to die. Everything crumbled around him. Then something strange happened; because death seemed so near, it took away from him the fear in every other area of his life. All of a sudden, he was making bold steps in his business. Because he was unafraid of losing everything in his business, he made bold steps he would never have under different circumstances. After all, what would a dying man have to lose?

If he chose to spend, he did it with absolutely no sense of fear or remorse. His mindset had shifted. Matthew could now afford to be vulnerable. He now had no problem risking it all. He was not afraid of rejection or the high probability that people would see his inadequacies. When Matthew kicked out fear, he gained everything he would ever have hoped for.

In his book, Allow, Matthew explains how people can move from struggling to get started to allowing the universe to deliver the results they seek. Because of the way he had been brought up, Matthew struggled to make success happen. He pushed every button he could think of to get himself to succeed, to no avail. He discovered that he was trying to do it with his own effort instead of allowing the universe to do it for him. As he began learning to let go and let the universe take over, things began to change. His hard work started paying off.

Matthew shares **THREE CRUCIAL STEPS** towards allowing prosperity into your life;

1. Follow your highest excitement in every moment.
2. Be true to yourself and do you.
   Don't follow a path that everyone else thinks is good for you. Whatever excites you, take the rules of whether it is good or bad out of it.
3. Embrace your dark side

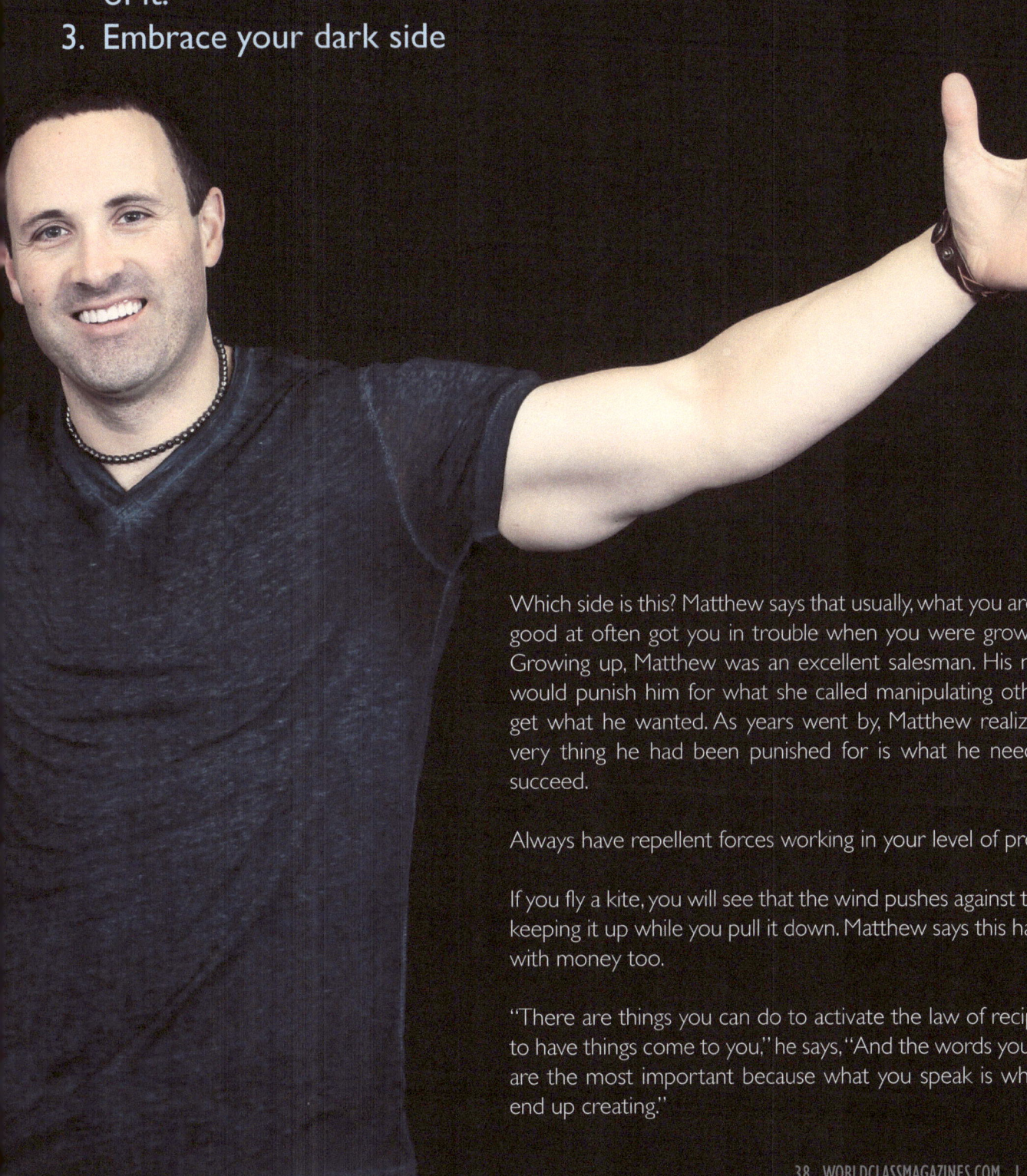

Which side is this? Matthew says that usually, what you are really good at often got you in trouble when you were growing up. Growing up, Matthew was an excellent salesman. His mother would punish him for what she called manipulating others to get what he wanted. As years went by, Matthew realized the very thing he had been punished for is what he needed to succeed.

Always have repellent forces working in your level of prosperity.

If you fly a kite, you will see that the wind pushes against the kite keeping it up while you pull it down. Matthew says this happens with money too.

"There are things you can do to activate the law of reciprocity to have things come to you," he says, "And the words you speak are the most important because what you speak is what you end up creating."

photo by FayeFaye Designs
make up for Veronica Grey by Espie Mapanao for Clinique

SUPERMODEL
VERONICA GREY:

LIVING LIFE WITH A PURPOSE
(Thanks to Justin Bieber).

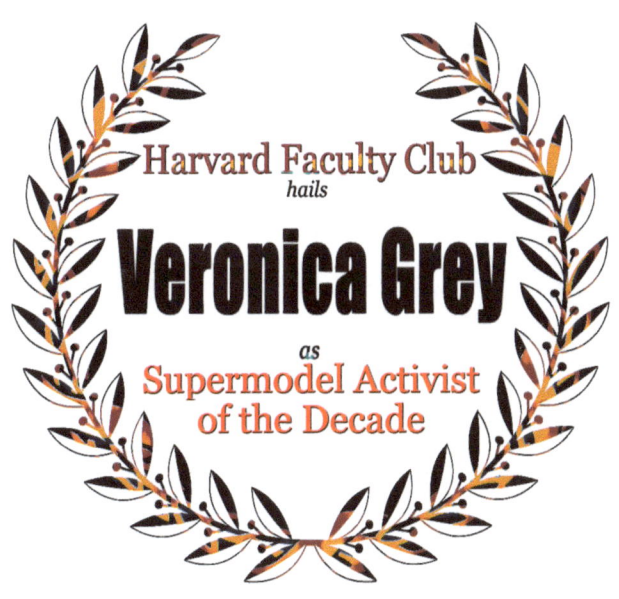

Fresh off Harvard naming her Supermodel Activist of the Decade, Veronica Grey may be happily influencing the Purpose Tour of Justin Bieber.

Ever steady in her path of Christ consciousness, when Veronica saw how impossible it was to bring every gift fans have for Justin with him on the tour, when there would be more gifts at the next stop, it was she who reminded an already altruistic Bieber that there are kids in hospitals who would benefit from those flowers and toys.

This is nothing new for Grey, which is why she is not merely the supermodel of the year, but of the decade, according to the Harvard Faculty Club presented by uber celebrity guru Clint Arthur and his lovely wife Alison Savitch.

Clint and Ali helm http://www.GuaranteedCelebrity.com which delivers exactly as it states with 100% success rate. They took an unknown barefoot hippy surf chick named Veronica Grey who couldn't be Googled five years ago and transformed her into the world's most televised surfer.

Now the media has branded her as the Queen of Surfing.
Yes it helps that she grew up with #1 surfer John John Florence, known as the King of Surfing.

And together John and Veronica have crowned Justin Bieber "Prince of Surfing."

Don't expect to catch Bieber on the waves any time soon as his global Purpose Tour extends to December. Veronica personally hopes it goes until next August 2017 and that, "Justin comes back home to Hawai'i with his full extravagant stage show."

With "Purpose" being his fourth bestselling album, Veronica is just one of many who Justin has influenced into living a life with "Purpose." It goes both ways for them.

It was probably her most recent award winning environmental documentary "Worst Shark Attack Ever" starring Leonardo DiCaprio, MGMT, The Cure, and John John Florence that catapulted Veronica Grey to A-list status.

photo of Veronica & John John by Said Shandala

Supermodel Veronica Grey photographed by National Geographic photographer Dotan Saguy.

She also directed "Aqua Seafoam Shame" (yes, that is a Nirvana lyric) which helped salvage the ocean from plastics. This documentary features Robert August of Endless Summer and music by The Cure and Depeche Mode.

It's not a big secret that the only meet and greet The Cure have ever had in the past few decades was to stage photos with the supermodel Veronica Grey. They perform in Hawai'i specifically so she doesn't have to come to them. Not that she minds.

"I get a lot done off band tours," Grey states. "The energy of these musicians have fueled four #1 bestselling books written by me and published through my not-for-profit organization Eternal Youth Empire."

The most recent one
Healthy, Wealthy, and Wise
The 5 Most Important Wellness Secrets of All Time has been promoted on major television networks like the CW and NBC.

So what's the Inside Scoop of the Purpose Tour with Justin Bieber?

"Well it's pretty funny," Veronica says. "When he sets foot outside it is like when boats throw bloody fish out in the ocean to go chumming for sharks. It's a feeding frenzy. The poor little rock star can't go out for ice cream unless he is hidden in the trunk of a car. When he goes out, I officially call it chumming," she laughs.

Maybe that's why Justin cancelled all remaining meet and greets for his Purpose Tour, although insiders say that he pretty much doesn't want to meet anyone else since he reconnected with long time friend Veronica Grey, who has been running around the rock and roll circus for years, being previously intimately involved with Billy Corgan of Smashing Pumpkins, Andrew Vanwyngarden of MGMT, and Oscar winning Jared Leto of Thirty Seconds to Mars.

But it was Justin Bieber and she who "won The Game together." Everyone else is just a close friend.

"Jared Leto and I met on the set of 'My So-Called Life' and knew each other before we were famous. It is such an honor and privilege to know that each and every Thirty Seconds to Mars album was partially inspired by our special friendship," explains Veronica, who is careful not to fall into the cliche' of rock stars who married supermodels.

"Yeah there are plenty of supermodels who married rock stars but I am one who uses my name to raise Christ consciousness on this planet. Maybe it's simply with a clean living vegetarian lifestyle of moderate temperance when it comes to alcohol," Grey finishes.

Either way all these supermodel rock star secrets that make you more attractive to members of the opposite sex including stopping or reversing the aging process can be found in her book
Healthy, Wealthy, and Wise
The 5 Most Important Wellness Secrets of All Time
http://www.amazon.com/gp/product/B00R8QP8MY
which went number one in half the countries that Amazon is even available.
So with four number one bestselling books and three award winning environmental documentaries under her belt, we can come to expect more from Veronica Grey for the remainder of the decade as its reigning super model.

"In the meanwhile I am happy to be paid to surf on TV shows like 'Hawai'i 5-0'and meeting my favorite musicians on tour, whether or not I am married to one."

The Cure are once again touring this year and you can be sure Veronica Grey will be in their audience on July 16 in Hawai'i and maybe other cities throughout May and June.

"And last time I was at Burning Man, Skrillex was there so maybe he'll be there again this year. I just wanna congratulate him, Diplo, and of course Justin Bieber for their recent Grammy win for 'Where Are You Now'."

Thank you Veronica Grey for letting us know where you are now. Namaste

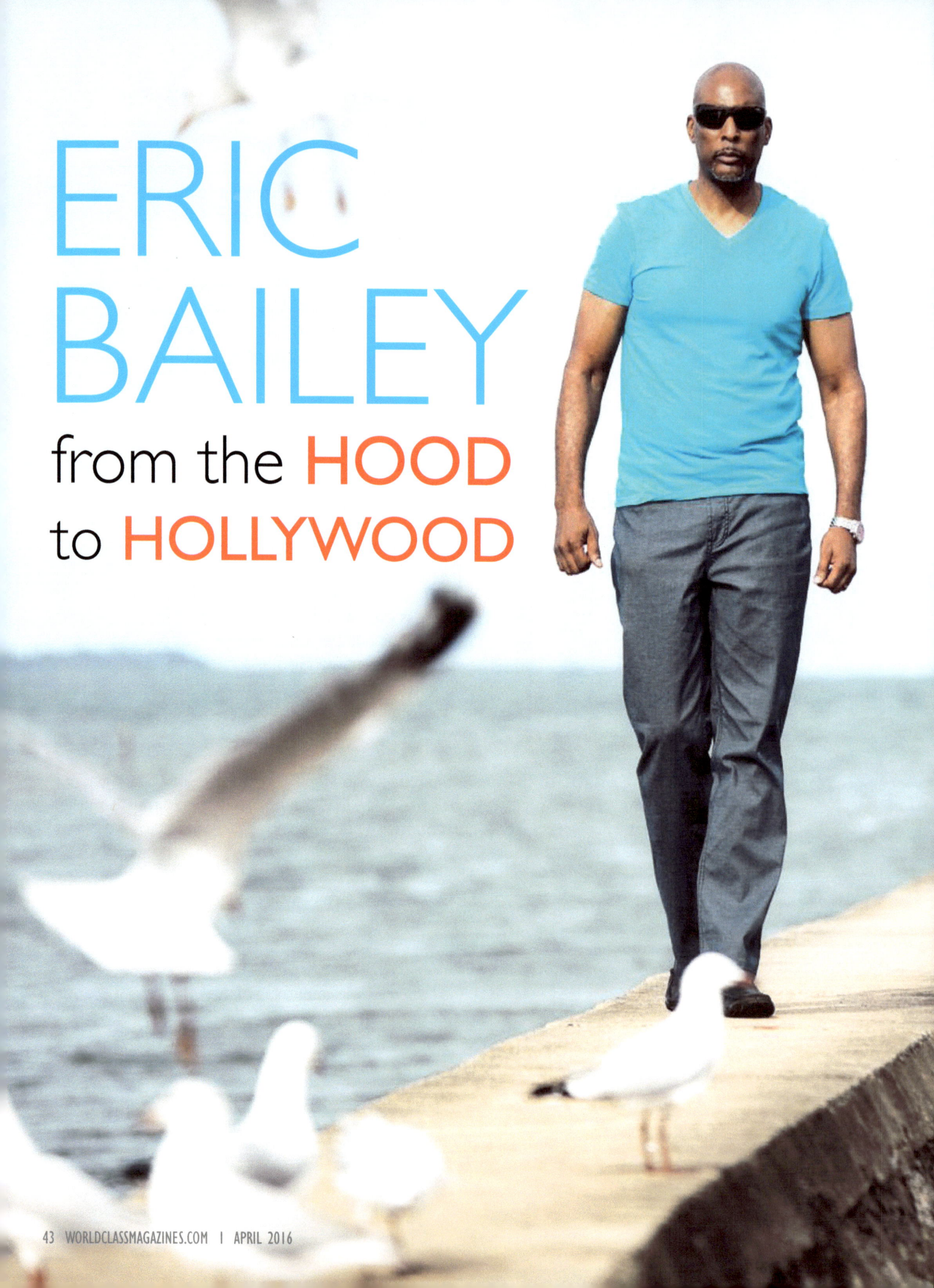

ERIC BAILEY
from the HOOD to HOLLYWOOD

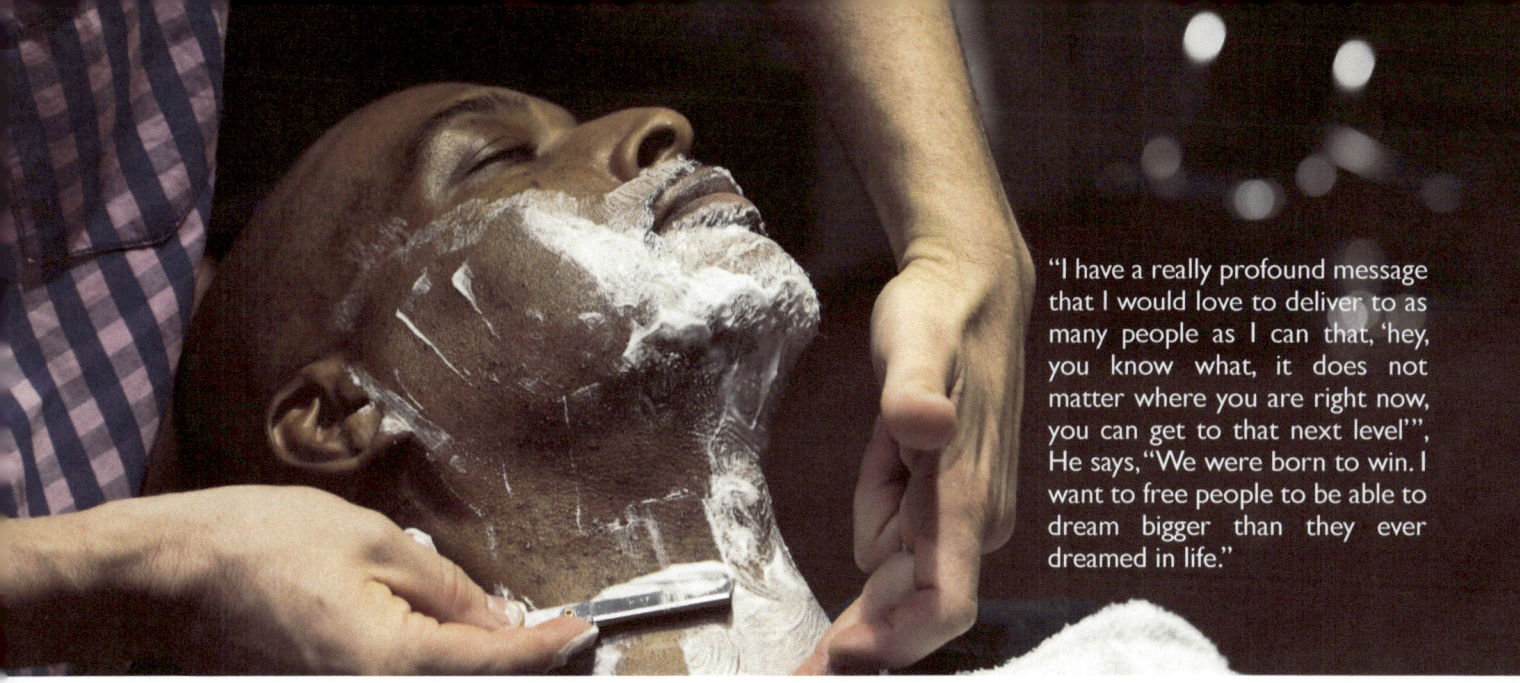

"I have a really profound message that I would love to deliver to as many people as I can that, 'hey, you know what, it does not matter where you are right now, you can get to that next level'", He says, "We were born to win. I want to free people to be able to dream bigger than they ever dreamed in life."

If you had told Eric Bailey that playing professional basketball would cost him as much as it did, he would have probably quit long before he got started. As a result of playing basketball, he has had nine knee operations, a hip replacement and chronic arthritis. But Eric also knows that if he had not gone through that pain, he would have been stuck in the hood and failed to become the person he is today. He says he was willing to go through whatever it took if it got him out of the hood and out of poverty.

Eric Bailey is a former professional basketball player and a Certified Speaking Professional (CSP). He is considered one of the world's most sought-after motivational speakers. Becoming a professional athlete is extremely hard, and very few people ever make it to professional sports.

Eric says to become a professional athlete he not only needed to be hardworking, skilled, dedicated and committed; he also needed to be passionate. He needed to be passionate enough to keep going even when times got hard.

Eric was brought up in south Los Angeles. His parents adopted him when they were in their forties. As a young person, Eric used to go to a barbershop near their home where he would polish people's shoes and get paid some money. He loved the conversations that were going on at the barbershop, ranging from politics, race, unemployment, travel. The conversations created a desire in him to want to get out of the neighborhood and travel the world.

Today, Eric works with companies and individuals to help them become the best in whatever they do. He coaches people to think like the best, for them to become the best. He presents a message of resilience and bouncing back emphasizing the need to embrace the mindset of a champion. His life is a testament that your race, your religion or your financial background does not have to dictate how your life pans out. And with everything going on in the United States today, Eric feels he has a message of freedom he can share with the nation.

Eric helps people identify within them their passion; what they could do even if they were not getting paid for it. He says that where your passion lies is where your ability is. Combining passion and ability creates purpose and with these three, taking action is inevitable.

For those people who struggle with motivating themselves to take action, Eric says they should create a daily playbook. This is a plan of things they must do every day for them to become successful. He says this plan will eventually become part of who they are and what they do. Eric says failure to create structure and disciple in the start of an action plan results in chaos. As a coach, he also holds people accountable for their action plan so that they can gain momentum and reach their set goals.

Eric's ideal client is anyone who is serious about making some improvements in their lives. He goes through a rigorous structure of identifying how serious his clients are. Over the past three years, he has mainly been dealing with corporate clients. He's worked with many Fortune 500 companies, including Procter and Gamble, Ford, McDonald's and Nike. He has specifically been helping people in the sales departments in various companies. He says selling is not just about the actual product that you're selling. It is also about selling yourself and your confidence. And coming from a sports background, he says he had learned to sell to his opponents his confidence, showing them that they needed to bring their 'A-game'.

Eric believes that we were all born to empower and enrich the lives of other people.

"When you can put other people's aspirations and goals a little bit higher on the priority list, then you allow yourself to give more of yourself. And when you can give more of yourself, it's just a good feeling," he says.

In goal-setting, Eric says people should set stupid goals; big, wild goals that will require you to work really hard to achieve them.

"Sometimes people set their goals and their goals really aren't high enough. Most people in life, they don't fail because they aimed high and missed, they fail in life because they aimed too low and they hit."

Eric's daily personal rituals involve getting up at 5 am every morning to go for a walk, ride a bike or go to the gym. He then takes breakfast, reads some books and listens to some audios. During the evening, he goes home, debriefs, chills and relaxes with his family. He loves spending his weekends with his family.

To Eric, success is hanging in there no matter the situations, circumstances, challenges, obstacles and pitfalls you may be facing. He defines greatness as doing what you have to do without stepping on anyone, harming anyone or compromising your values and beliefs.

In a period of just a month, Eric wrote his book "Bring Your A-Game". The book is about helping people take their game to the next level. He wants to help people gain consistency and momentum. At the time when he was writing the book, he was at a low place. He had just lost a major international position with a company, his beautiful dog of 18 years had died and he had a cancer scare.

As he wondered why all these things were happening to him, he looked at his life and realized that he was supposed to use whatever he was going through to write the book. He wrote the book while still hurting. He says he would be typing with tears rolling down his face. In the book, he has highlighted 12 A's that have been very prevalent for him. Some of the A's include abandonment, adoption, attitude, and accelerate.

The book will be released in February, 2016 and will be available on Amazon. It will also be available on his website:
http://ericbaileyglobal.com/

DR. JOSEPH MINA
ATALLA
SPECTACULAR SMILE

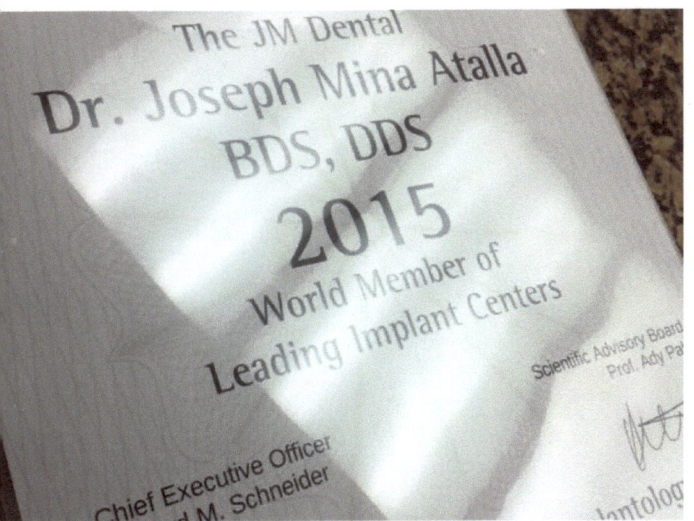

Dr Joseph Mina Atalla's approach to creating the perfect smile is unique and different. Most dentists would tell you to go for that white and symmetrical look. Dr Joseph wouldn't. To Dr Joseph, the decision is not that obvious. He says white and symmetrical is great but not always spectacular. With every one of his patients, Dr Atalla seeks to do what would best serve them. His aim is not to just give his patients a white smile, but a smile that best matches how they look and their personality. He considers the patient's complexion, his hair color, the color of his eyes and even the color of their hair. He believes that sometimes it is a good idea to add a little touch of uniqueness to a smile creating a smile that is more accurate to the person's personality.

> **"We don't all speak the same; we don't all have the same tone of voice; we don't all smile the same. So as long as we are all unique, all smiles sometimes have to have a touch of uniqueness,"** he says.

There is hardly anything ordinary about Dr Joseph Mina Atalla. His unique approach to situations did not begin when he established his dental practice in Santa Ana, California. His life is full of examples of thinking outside the box and looking at life scenarios with a different set of eyes. By the time he celebrated his 22nd birthday, he was already a dentist. He has studied dentistry in four different countries including Germany, the United States, Britain, and Mexico. He speaks English, French, Spanish and Arabic and is a member of five professional bodies including California Dental Association and International Congress of Oral Implantologists. His areas of expertise include general dentistry, cosmetic dentistry, and dental pain.

It is perhaps this approach to life that has made it needful that he does something special for every patient that walks through his doors. The process of identifying the smile that would be best suited to them is quite interesting. Dr Joseph asks his patient the kind of beauty they are looking for. As the patient speaks, he observes the way he speaks and how many of their teeth are showing. He then gives him the option of adding a touch of uniqueness that would bring out the kind of smile they are known for.

White teeth are always an option, but Dr Joseph says some patients are usually looking for something different. They don't want the typical smile that everyone else has. Veneers and implants are the big part of Dr Joseph's practice. They also do crowns. Their ideal patient is someone who is looking for a really big smile as well as someone who appreciates their own smile and wants to enhance it. Dr Joseph is not big on white, piano, straight teeth. While having white, piano, straight teeth is beautiful, Dr Joseph appreciates patients who have a sense of art in trying to achieve something new.

Dr Joseph usually gives his patients one or two consultations to determine what they are looking for. He then gives them his opinion regarding their teeth and presents the different options available to them to enhance their teeth and smile. From there, he implements the plan they have agreed with the patient. He schedules around three to four dental visits for people who have lost their feet and are in need of implants and crowns.

For veneers, a patient is usually free to continue eating normally but for implants, sometimes a patient has to wait for three to four months before he can go back to eating normally. This period is to allow the bone around the teeth to heal and grow around the implants. There are, however, certain cases of implants where a patient can be allowed to continue with their normal eating habits.

Enhancing the smile of a person has enormous positive psychological effects on the person. A beautiful smile allows people to smile more often; it gives them the confidence to go out and allows them to show confidence during interviews.

"There is nothing that warms the heart more than a nice, thick and warm smile," says Dr Atalla.

If you have been considering a new smile, Dr Atalla says you should not be afraid. The whole process begins with a walk into their offices for help. He also encourages them to be open to the idea of something beautiful and unique to them.

To get in touch with Dr Joseph Atalla, you can visit their offices at 801 N Tustin Avenue, Suite 708, Santa Ana, CA, 92705. His practice is called The JM Dental. The office phone number is 714-285-0500.

Whether you are looking for a huge smile or just an ideal smile, The JM Dental has a perfect solution to help you smile more often and showcase your personality.

CAMIE J. CARPENTER
HOLLYWOOD TALENT MAKER

Her clients' current credits include co-starring roles on the soap operas All My Children and The Young and the Restless, HBO's True Detective and Entourage, AMC's Mad Men, ABC's Scandal, CBS's NCIS and Criminal Minds, Nickelodeon's Victorious, Disney's Jessie and a recurring Guest Star role on Lab Rats. Principal roles in national commercials for Little Caesars, McDonalds, Wendy's, Samsung, Disneyland, MasterCard, Pepsi, Chevrolet and Lens Crafters in addition to print campaigns for Guess, H&M, LG, Sony, Allergan, Gap, Children's Place, Target, Neiman Marcus, Abercrombie & Fitch, American Apparel. Her clients have appeared in films that have been screened at Cannes Film Festival and Sundance Film Festival and have been featured in the 2016 Oscar Nominated film, Straight Outta Compton.

Nestled away in the village of the hillside seaside community of La Jolla, California some 90 miles from the glitz and glam of Los Angeles, the entertainment capital of the world is the office of Talent Manager, Camie Carpenter, who represents almost 300 credited film/TV actors (imdb.com) in addition to her stable of models and commercial talent, ranging in age from six months to mid-eighties.

"I cannot promise fame and fortune," says Camie, **who is brutally honest to prospective talent when first come to see her, "I can't do the work for you,"** she explains, **"But this really like any business, but in this case it just happens to be you."**

With a BA in Communications with an emphasis in Marketing from the University of Southern California, she was cherry picked by a Fortune 50 Company for a major account position, being one of only three women in an elite division of 200 nationally. The beauty industry was her next stop, doubling sales within a year and a half for the division she directed nationally, Revlon recently bought the company.

"The question everyone always asks me how I got into this business," says Camie, **"Well I was sitting in the lobby of my office reading the paper and this guy walking in and said, you should be in show business, I started laughing, but it turned out he managed up and coming talent and was looking for office space. Long story short here we are over a decade later."**

I was lucky enough to stop by on a day that Michaela Carrozza who plays Catlin on Disney's Lab Rats was also in the office. Michaela has been in the business for the past seven years, she began her career in theatre, her first TV credit was a recurring Guest Star role on Nickelodeon's iCarly and has had principal roles in national commercials for McDonalds and Coke Zero to name a few. Michaela's advice, "I believe if you set your mind to something, you can accomplish anything," well she is certainly doing that as a successful actress. Camie meets with her clients on a regular basis for updates on what they have been doing; auditions, keeping up with social networking, industry events, updating the resume, red carpet events, updating photos and then like any manager reviews short and long term making sure talent is on track.

Another client of Camie's, Merrick McCartha, who has appeared as a Co-star on six network shows, explains he didn't know anything about the business when he got started, but walked into Camie's office, **"She helped me, she guided me, she really got me going and still gives me a lot of opportunities for work and I really appreciate her always."**

Her clients are also involved in the industry in other ways as well, Casey Robinson is the Vice President, SAG-AFTRA San Diego Local, Sarah Merritt-Eastman is the Vice President of the National Board of Review and Dr. Judy Bauerlein is the Dean for the Theatre Department at Cal State, San Marcos.

She represents all walks of life from Surgeons, Lawyers, Dentists, Professional Athletes, Tennis Pros, Wealth Advisors, Engineers, Authors, Sommeliers, Life Coaches, Business Owners, School Teachers, Bartenders, College Students, Active Duty Military, Construction Workers, Retail Sales Clerks, Yoga Teachers, Personal Trainers, News Reporters, Radio Personalities, Housewives, Car Wash Attendants, Law Enforcement, Firemen, YouTubers, Instagrammers, retired people, kids and teens, you get the idea, Camie says, **"Anyone can do this at some level as long as there is an interest and a desire to."**

Besides working with professional talent and those just started out, her priority is building relationships, her office and cell phone ring off the hook. Sam Warren, CSA (Casting Society of America) called about a new project and Tom Logan, DGA (Director Guild of America) called to check her schedule for April. Tom is a member of the Academy which votes for the Emmy Awards and the Oscars. She tells Tom to say something nice about her and hands me the phone, I remember Tom from General Hospital he was on the show for eight years before he moved into Directing.

"Camie's devotion to her clients is sincere and ethical. She opens doors for her talent and obtains opportunities that might possibly secure their big breaks. Having said that, it's up to the actors to follow through. I, as the industry as a whole, am so blessed to work with people like Camie. She is a credit to the entertainment industry," says Tom.

In 2006 Camie cast her first short film, her clients CG Thomas and Gerren Hall have given her the opportunity to also get in front camera building her acting credits just as she tells her clients to do, in addition she does a bit of commercial print modeling.

"Being on set really helps give me insight into what my clients go through," says Camie, "But I prefer the life as a Talent Manger for now."

To keep up with the on goings of Camie's talent follow @htacasting on Instagram and Twitter, also do not forget to like Hollywood Talent Associates Facebook Fanpage.

Most of Dr. Nalluri's patients are referred to him by his former patients and doctors across Florida. His excellence in the field of plastic surgery has made him a sought-after plastic surgeon. Unlike some doctors who practice plastic surgery, Dr. Raja Nalluri has undergone extensive training in the field. He is board-certified by the American Board of Plastic Surgery, perhaps the hardest certification to attain for any plastic surgeon. In addition, he uses excellent techniques he experienced from world renowned physicians, making sure he achieves great results without compromising the safety of the patient.

This is perhaps why he hardly does any advertising. His plastic surgery practice is not a gamble resulting from doing a few courses. Most people would rather visit a fully certified plastic surgeon with extensive training and numerous certifications.

In addition to this, Dr. Nalluri has been rated as one of the top doctors by Castle Connolly and U.S. News & World Report, independent agencies that rate doctors based on their quality. This type of recognition by independent agencies is not something you can buy. Other prestigious awards bestowed on Dr. Nalluri include America's Best Physicians and Cosmopolitan Magazine's Top Plastic Surgeons in Florida.

When asked how he manages to keep his life in balance, Nalluri responds: "Felicia, my best friend, my surgical assistant and the love of my life is the one person who is always there for me."

As a result of his excellent reputation, many patients contact him through his website. Dr. Nalluri does not believe in doing as many procedures as possible. Instead of quantity, Dr. Nalluri prefers to have a manageable number of patients. That way, he can take enough time with each patient to make sure the results are exactly as desired.

"My practice is not run like a factory, where we are doing a large number of cases each day. It's something where each individual I take individual time and give them sort of that individual attention," says the doctor. Dr. Nalluri's father was a doctor and inspired him immensely. Growing up in Youngstown, Ohio he wanted to be just like his dad. When he went to medical school at Case Western Reserve University in Cleveland, Ohio he got to experience the different fields. He fell in love with plastic surgery. Dr. Nalluri says he loved the immediate satisfaction he could provide for his patients. He also says he loved the fact that plastic surgery is artistic, challenging and rewarding. In plastic surgery, you are also not confined in a box; sometimes you have to create and use your thinking to come up with a solution for individual patients.

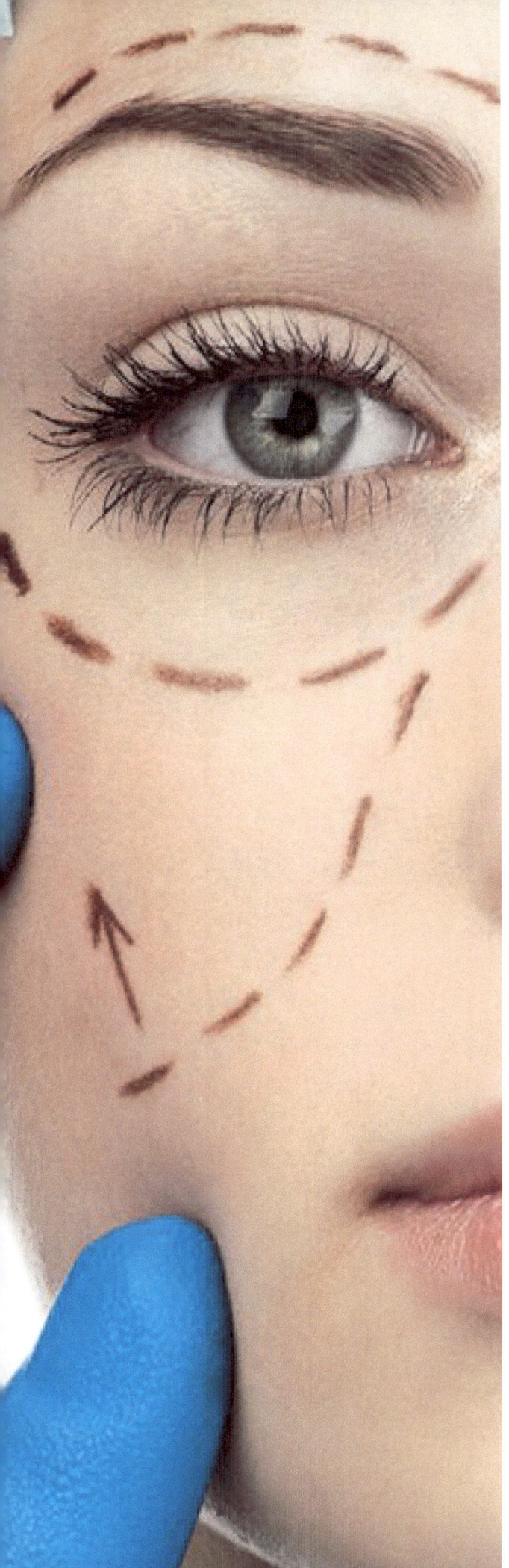

Dr. Nalluri used to play tennis in high school. He used to visit Florida for tennis training and games. After experiencing the area, he liked it. When he had a chance to finish his training, there was no doubt in his mind that the best place to go to start his career was Florida.

Today, Dr. Nalluri's most popular procedures include breast augmentation, liposuction, tummy tuck, and facelifts. His patients range from teenagers to middle-aged mothers who may want restoration of their breast and abdomen anatomy. He also serves the older generation that is looking to deal with sagging eyelids and such other age-related issues.

Dr. Nalluri takes around an hour with each patient. This time allows him to listen to their expectations and concerns as well as understand their needs. He also takes the time to show them sample results of his past work and help them understand the process. He also gives them educational materials they can go through before undergoing whichever procedure they are seeking for. Different procedures take varied lengths of time for the patient to heal and go back to performing their day to day activities. Laser procedures, peels, and injections, for instance, have little to no recovery time. Some of them can be done over lunch and the patient is able to go back to work. Procedures that use general anesthesia like facelifts, breast and abdomen procedures take a week or two. Full body makeovers usually take a little over two weeks.

To slow down aging, good health habits are a must. Before you consider surgery, it is important to practice good nutrition, avoid smoking, minimize exposure to sunlight, and employ a good skin regimen. These simple practices can drastically slow down aging. Dr. Nalluri also says it is important to avoid large weight gains and losses. Beyond this, there are other circumstances that make it needful that someone undergoes a procedure to deal with these signs of aging. These include skin laxity from pregnancy or weight loss or signs of aging as a result of their genetics. Dr. Nalluri says before making the decision to go through plastic surgery, it is important that you seek a number of expert opinions. He says some doctors say they are board certified without mentioning which board has certified them.

"...look for that board certification by the American Board of Plastic Surgery."

"The only board that is requiring the amount of training to really have a surgeon be capable of performing these procedures faithfully and effectively is the American Board of Plastic Surgery," he says, **"Other boards may simply be as simple as applying and paying a fee and taking a weekend course."**

Dr. Nalluri's daily routines include running, and weight-lifting. He is a fitness advocate who received a Presidential Academic Fitness Award and was Valedictorian in 1989.

To get in touch with Dr. Nalluri, you can visit his website at www.nalluri.com.

You can also call this number: 941-752-7842 (941-PLASTIC). For patients far away, he has FaceTime and Skype consultations.

Due to the popularity of plastic surgery, it has become commonplace for people to go to whichever doctor that is offering the lowest price or the most advertising. Dr. Nalluri says this is leading to patients who are either misinformed or uninformed, creating unnecessary trouble and complications. He urges patients to look for that board certification by the American Board of Plastic Surgery.

5 ways to stay motivated

One of the most challenging parts of being productive and successful all comes down to finding ways to stay motivated. If you are someone who easily gets and stays motivated, this skill can be one of your greatest tools. If you are someone who struggles with motivation, it can be one of your biggest obstacles.

It may seem hard to stay motivated when you keep working but feel like you are not getting anywhere. In these situations, it is more important than ever to find the strength and focus needed to push past the challenging time and to really stay motivated.

Here are five ways you can stay motivated, even when it seems like your efforts aren't getting you anywhere:

1. START BY KNOWING YOUR MOTIVATING FORCE

Everyone has their own different motivating force or factor and they can vary from person-to-person. In order to stay motivated even in the most challenging of times you need to know what your individual motivating force is. You need to have a reason to succeed.

What is your reason for wanting to keep going? What is your reason to keep working even if you aren't seeing the results that you want? You need to know what motivates you. What is your big picture goal that put you on this path in the first place? If you can channel what this is, then you will have the strength and vision to stay motivated no matter what comes your way. "The experience of pain or loss can be a formidably motivating force." – John C. Maxwell

2. KNOW WHAT YOU CAN LOSE

Sometimes just knowing what you want isn't enough to really motivate you. There are many people who react better to knowing what they can lose. If you are struggling to stay motivated because you aren't seeing the rewards or benefits that you want, start focusing on what you could lose by giving up. What will happen if you don't keep going? This outcome may just be the boost you need to push forward.about what other people are saying or thinking about you and your situation and instead let it go. It can help you regain focus and help you get back to the motivated place you want to be.

GET YOURSELF ORGANIZED

When you are extremely busy and are dealing with a cluttered over-stimulated brain, it can easily not only ruin your focus but your energy as well. It can seem almost impossible to stay motivated and push past certain challenges when you are dealing with a cluttered and organized brain.

Take a moment to really write out all of your thoughts and ideas and get them organized. Many times, just taking a moment to organize your thoughts can give you the clarity that you need to make the right decisions and to find the motivation to keep going.

Taking some pressure off your brain by moving your thoughts to a more organized list is a great way to unload, unwind and regain the focus you need to find the motivation you desire.

BE READY WITH A BACKUP PLAN

Many times people find they are not reaching their desired outcome, not because they don't have the right skills or talents, but because they don't have the right approach. Instead of getting down on yourself and losing steam when things don't seem to be working out, try a new approach and come up with a new plan.

Be prepared to change courses. It doesn't mean giving up, it means starting over with a different approach to the same problem. Sometimes a fresh perspective is all you need to find success and the renewed energy and motivation required to meet your goals.

Thomas Edison once said it best when he claimed he's never failed he's just "found 10,000 ways that won't work." You may not need to try out 10,000 approaches, but having a backup plan or two can only help you regain your feelings of motivation.

LET IT GO

In the words of the now famous Disney song, sometimes you just need to let it go. There are so many people that find a block in their motivation not because they don't want to keep pushing on, but because something they are holding on to is getting in the way. If you find that you get easily upset or frustrated, or are worried about what other people are thinking about your shortcomings, let it go.

"Some of us think holding on makes us strong; but sometimes it is letting go." – Hermann Hesse

Feelings like this can only leave you feeling pre-occupied and unfocused. Don't worry so much about what other people are saying or thinking about you and your situation and instead let it go. It can help you regain focus and help you get back to the motivated place you want to be.

Credit: addicted2success.com

"Some of us think holding on makes us strong; but sometimes it is letting go."

– Hermann Hesse

21 Tips

to

BECOME THE MOST PRODUCTIVE PERSON YOU KNOW

(by Robin Sharma)

I wanted to help you create explosive productivity so you get big things done (and make your life matter).

Here are 21 tips to get you to your best productivity.

1 Check email in the afternoon so you protect the peak energy hours of your mornings for your best work.

2 Stop waiting for perfect conditions to launch a great project. Immediate action fuels a positive feedback loop that drives even more action.

3 Remember that big, brave goals release energy. So set them clearly and then revisit them every morning for 5 minutes.

4 Mess creates stress (I learned this from tennis icon Andre Agassi who said he wouldn't let anyone touch his tennis bag because if it got disorganized, he'd get distracted). So clean out the clutter in your office to get more done.

5 Sell your TV. You're just watching other people get successful versus doing the things that will get you to your dreams.

6 Say goodbye to the energy vampires in your life (the negative souls who steal your enthusiasm).

7 Run routines. When I studied the creative lives of massively productive people like Stephen King, John Grisham and Thomas Edison, I discovered they follow strict daily routines. (i.e., when they would get up, when they would start work, when they would exercise and when they would relax). Peak productivity's not about luck. It's about devotion.

8 Get up at 5 am. Win the battle of the bed. Put mind over mattress. This habit alone will strengthen your willpower so it serves you more dutifully in the key areas of your life.

9 Don't do so many meetings. (I've trained the employees of our FORTUNE 500 clients on exactly how to do this – including having the few meetings they now do standing up – and it's created breakthrough results for them).

10 Don't say yes to every request. Most of us have a deep need to be liked. That translates into us saying yes to everything – which is the end of your elite productivity.

11 Outsource everything you can't be BIW (Best in the World) at. Focus only on activities within what I call "Your Picasso Zone".

12 Stop multi-tasking. New research confirms that all the distractions invading our lives are rewiring the way our brains work (and drop our IQ by 5 points!). Be one of the rare-air few who develops the mental and physical discipline to have a monomaniacal focus on one thing for many hours. (It's all about practice).

13 Get fit like Madonna. Getting to your absolute best physical condition will create explosive energy, renew your focus and multiply your creativity.

14   Workout 2 X a day. This is just one of the little-known productivity tactics that I'll walk you through in my new online training program YOUR PRODUCTIVITY UNLEASHED (details at the end of this post) but here's the key: exercise is one of the greatest productivity tools in the world. So do 20 minutes first thing in the morning and then another workout around 6 or 7 pm to set you up for wow in the evening.

15   Drink more water. When you're dehydrated, you'll have far less energy and get less done.

16   Work in 90-minute blocks with 10-minute intervals to recover and refuel (another game-changing move I personally use to do my best work).

17   Write a Stop Doing List. Every productive person obsessively sets To Do Lists. But those who play at world-class also record what they commit to stop doing. Steve Jobs said that what made Apple was not so much what they chose to build but all the projects they chose to ignore.

18   Use your commute time. If you're commuting 30 minutes each way every day – get this: at the end of a year, you've spent 6 weeks of 8 hour days in your car. I encourage you to use that time to listen to fantastic books on audio + excellent podcasts and valuable learning programs. Remember, the fastest way to double your income is to triple your rate of learning.

19   Be a contrarian. Why buy your groceries at the time the store is busiest? Why go to movies on the most popular nights? Why hit the gym when the gym's completely full? Do things at off-peak hours and you'll save so many of them.

20   Get things right the first time. Most people are wildly distracted these days. And so they make mistakes. To unleash your productivity, become one of the special performers who have the mindset of doing what it takes to get it flawless first. This saves you days of having to fix problems.

21   Get lost. Don't be so available to everyone. I often spend hours at a time in the cafeteria of a university close to our headquarters. I turn off my devices and think, create, plan and write. Zero interruptions. Pure focus. Massive results.

http://www.robinsharma.com

Inspirational Life Quotes

"Just know, when you truly want success, you'll never give up on it.
No matter how bad the situation may get." – *Unknown*

"Accept responsibility for your life.
Know that it is you who will get you where you want to go, no one else." – *Les Brown*

"I don't regret the things I've done, I regret the things I didn't do when I had the chance." – *Unknown*

"Challenges are what make life interesting and overcoming them is what makes life meaningful."
– *Joshua J. Marine*

"Its hard to wait around for something you know might never happen;
but its harder to give up when you know its everything you want." – *Unknown*

"One of the most important keys to Success is having the discipline to do what you know you should do,
even when you dont feel like doing it." – *Unknown*

"Good things come to those who wait…
greater things come to those who get off their ass and do anything to make it happen." – *Unknown*

"Happiness cannot be traveled to, owned, earned, or worn.
It is the spiritual experience of living every minute with love, grace & gratitude." – *Denis Waitley*

"In order to succeed, your desire for success should be greater than your fear of failure." – *Bill Cosby*

"Go where you are celebrated – not tolerated.
If they can't see the real value of you, it's time for a new start." – *Unknown*
Dont be afraid to stand for what you believe in, even if that means standing alone. – *Unknown*

"The best revenge is massive success." – *Frank Sinatra*

"Forget all the reasons it won't work and believe the one reason that it will." – *Unknown*

"I am thankful for all of those who said NO to me. Its because of them I'm doing it myself." – *Albert Einstein*

"The only way to do great work is to love what you do.
If you haven't found it yet, keep looking. Don't settle." – *Steve Jobs*

"Life is short, live it. Love is rare, grab it. Anger is bad, dump it.
Fear is awful, face it. Memories are sweet, cherish it." – *Unknown*

"When you say "It's hard", it actually means "I'm not strong enough to fight for it".
Stop saying its hard. Think positive!" – *Unknown*

"Life is like photography. You need the negatives to develop." – *Unknown*

"Don't worry about failures, worry about the chances you miss when you don't even try." – *Jack Canfield*

"The pain you feel today is the strength you feel tomorrow.
For every challenge encountered there is opportunity for growth." – *Unknown*

"Build your own dreams, or someone else will hire you to build theirs." – *Farrah Gray*

"The only thing that stands between you and your dream is the will to try
and the belief that it is actually possible." – *Joel Brown*

"Self confidence is the most attractive quality a person can have.
How can anyone see how awesome you are if you can't see it yourself?" – *Unknown*

"We learn something from everyone who passes through our lives.
Some lessons are painful, some are painless.. but, all are priceless." – *Unknown*

"Being happy doesn't mean that everything is perfect.
It means that you've decided to look beyond the imperfections." – *Unknown*

"Nobody ever wrote down a plan to be broke, fat, lazy, or stupid.
Those things are what happen when you don't have a plan." – *Larry Winget*

"Three things you cannot recover in life: the WORD after it's said,
the MOMENT after it's missed and the TIME after it's gone. Be Careful!" – *Unknown*

"Though no one can go back and make a brand new start,
anyone can start from now and make a brand new ending." – *Carl Bard*

"When the past calls, let it go to voicemail, believe me, it has nothing new to say." – *Unknown*

"Rule #1 of life. Do what makes YOU happy." – *Unknown*

"Walk away from anything or anyone who takes away from your joy.
Life is too short to put up with fools." – *Unknown*

"Love what you have. Need what you want. Accept what you receive. Give what you can.
Always remember, what goes around, comes around…" – *Unknown*

"Just remember there is someone out there that is more than happy with less than what you have."
– *Unknown*

"The biggest failure you can have in life is making the mistake of never trying at all." – *Unknown*

"Life has two rules: #1 Never quit #2 Always remember rule # 1." – *Unknown*

"No one is going to hand me success. I must go out & get it myself. That's why I'm here.
To dominate. To conquer. Both the world, and myself." – *Unknown*

*We hope you enjoyed these inspirational life quotes today.
Please don't forget to share these with your friends, family and followers to brighten their day
and inspire them to live a better life.*

www.ingramcontent.com/pod-product-compliance
Lightning Source LLC
Chambersburg PA
CBHW050741180526
45159CB00003B/1309